Your Touch Can Heal

(Revised 1998)

Malcolm H. Miner

ISBN:978-0-9848679-0-5

Library of Congress Catalog Card #92-072804

Other Books by Malcolm Miner:

Healing Is For Real (©Copyright 1972,
Morehouse-Barlow Co. New York, N.Y.)

Healing And The Abundant Life (©Copyright 1979,
Morehouse-Barlow Co. Wilton, CT)

Dedication

I should like to dedicate this book to those who have experienced the **Healing Touch** with me. First of these is my wife Imogene who shares **touch** with me on a daily basis. Then there are my children, Donna and Linda, upon whom I first practiced my healing art, and my son Phil, who later on shared the healing gifts with me. There are people like Peter Somers, who encouraged me to publish this book, and Dan and Lisa who came by as we were working on it. And I must include the countless others through the years, who helped me to learn by letting me practice **touch** on them. Then there are those for whom touch was the final victory over disease, Joan, Gena and Bud, and most recently, Andy and my dear friend, Mary Mildred Jones, who have moved on to new lives of perfect service.

PREFACE

When I signed up for an attitudinal healing workshop led by Dr. Bernie Siegel, Dr. Gerald Jampolsky, Dr. Donald Pachuta and Dianne Cirincione, I was introduced to some new concepts. I had been working with the Order of St. Luke, a Christian organization which emphasizes the value of the spiritual methods as a source of healing. These doctors, who were talking about applying their medical techniques with love and compassion in an atmosphere of hope, seemed to be talking the same language. For forty years as an Episcopal priest I had been teaching that a loving and caring spirit was the cornerstone of healing. Their seminar both affirmed me and offered me a broader dimension than the Church alone. I felt that I was their partner in a cause that was larger than either the Church or medicine. The leaders of the workshop mentioned above expressed the love of God as taught by Jesus, fully as much as I had done in my many years in the ministry. I saw that if all of us in the healing arts could cooperate with one another, that we should achieve greater results in healing.

After retirement from my work in Alaska I moved to the island of Kauai in the Hawaiian chain, the place where I had attended the seminar mentioned above. Soon after taking up residence here I became involved with some of the physicians nurses and lay persons working with attitudinal healing. My wife, Imogene, and I have developed a working relationship with oncologist, Dr. Neal Sutherland and his wife, Linda, who is a nurse as well as an ordained Deacon in the Episcopal Church. They, along with Dr. Donald Pachuta, who has become a resident here, have allowed me and my wife to share in their work and participate in their conferences. Siegel continues to be involved with our local efforts as he makes periodic visits here for rest and relaxation. Kauai is an island of beauty where one can daily experience the majesty of God in his fullness. It is an atmosphere where the healing gifts flourish in everyone. We are busy, we are involved with more growth experiences and more experiences and more opportunities to serve both in the churches and in the communities here .

In the preparation of this book I am particularly indebted to my loving wife, my partner in life and best friend, Imogene Hagensen Miner, for her help, advice and encouragement to me with the present book. She reviewed the chapters as they were being written and in addition to doing the proof reading, she gave me many helpful suggestions for the final manuscript. She is at the same time my student and my teacher.

I am also indebted to my friend, the Rev. Jan Rudinoff, Rector of St Michael and All' Angels, our church here on this island. Jan made many helpful suggestions while I was editing the manuscript. I am also indebted to my friends, Peter Somers, for his assistance in the editing process. Peter learned about the "healing touch" personally as one healed from a serious illness. I should also like to include my friend of many years Fr. Bernard Van Waes, O.H.C. for going over my manuscript and sharing his ideas.

Those of you who have heard me at conferences will find a familiar ring to these writings as I have borrowed substantially from my talks . I teach by telling stories from out of my personal experiences. I find that I witness best to those things I have seen and heard in my own life They cover the entire range of experiences from my earliest days in ministry through my many years in Alaska up to my present activities here in Hawaii. I find that as long as we remain active in the arena of life the Holy Spirit gives us new experiences daily - experiences to teach us, to encourage us and to make our work more effective. Life goes on...it is good.

    I always have to thank my children, Linda, Donna and Phil for giving me their love, support and friendship, and ideas for my talks, for without them and their impact on me, I might not have much to say.

        Malcolm H. Miner
        Brennecke's Beach at Poipu,
        Island of Kauai, Hawaii

TABLE OF CONTENTS

Chapter 1
The Magic of Touch

YOUR TOUCH CAN HEAL. That is what this book is all about. You are already a healer - without even trying. Without even knowing it you have already healed people with your touch. It does not matter how old you are, your sex, your religious beliefs or your lack of them, your touch can heal. Healing touch is a natural attribute shared by all human beings.

Touch is important. It is necessary for life. It is necessary for health. From birth our mother's touch is a primary factor in our nurture. It is our first contact with other members of the human family. It never stops being important to us. It can mean the difference between life and death. Christi's story is an example of this.

Christi entered this world suffering from a number of handicaps. She was born with Goldenhar Syndrome, a condition affecting one half of the body. When she was a day old she underwent surgery to free one of her lungs, so it could function properly. Somehow, some of her intestines had moved up to that part of her body. During the surgery her heart had stopped, which worried the doctors, because of the threat of brain damage. I was asked by the family to baptize their baby because her life was hanging by a thread. As I touched her, she appeared to take on a new strength. Her behavior encouraged me to cheer her on. Each time I visited the hospital and prayed for her from outside a glass barrier, she continued to rally. As I prayed to God I also sent messages to her, "Come on, Christi, you can do it", and she would respond by moving around and kicking.

However, the atmosphere in that place was all gloom and doom. Because of a breathing problem she was kept on a respirator. No one, including her mother, was able to hold her. One nurse said to me," I hope that you're praying for her to die, because if she lives, she'll only be a vegetable". We seemed to be at a standstill. I felt she should be moved to different surroundings and our prayer group prayed for that. My hopes were realized when another physician entered the picture. He moved her to a hospital run by the Sisters of Providence, where a great emphasis is placed on touch and loving care. One of the first things they did was to remove her from the respirator periodically so that she could be nurtured with human touch. Now Christi could be held by her mother and receive the bonding she needed. There the nurses gave her lots of hands on treatment as well. She thrived on this program of loving touch and gained more strength with each day and soon was taken off of the respirator completely. The only change in therapy was the nurturing touch that heals and it made the difference between life and death. Yes, Christi was healed. The baby who some were ready to write off became a beautiful young person, bright- eyed, intelligent and full of love - a joy to her family and friends.

From Christi's case I learned some things about writing people off because they might not make it in the world according to some people's expectations. People do that all the time with Down's Syndrome babies and others born with handicaps. Think of all the joy and excitement that has come with the Special Olympics because someone has seen the possibilities in these persons. Years ago, my first child, Harold, was born with

Down's Syndrome. At that time, no encouragement was given to us concerning our child. We were told that he was "hopelessly incurable", and that we shouldn't get too close to him for our own sakes, because we'd eventually have to give him up.

We did have to give him up, but God had something special in mind for him. Harold had to be hospitalized because of a severe respiratory problem. He was placed in a state hospital for children with physical and mental handicaps and was the only baby in the hospital. The teen-age girls who were permanent patients, were allowed to care for little Harold, to cradle him as their own baby. He loved it. Though he lived only nine months, he received the blessings of being touched frequently by these loving, surrogate mothers. Through them he experienced the joy of being accepted, appreciated and loved.

During World War II, a number of children in England were born out of wedlock, the offspring of servicemen who were stationed there. These children were placed in orphanages where there were too few nurses to care for them. When it was noted that many were doing poorly, even to the extent of dying, the doctors looked for a cause. The cause was lack of touch. There simply were not enough nurses to pick up and physically handle these babies. Once this was discovered, a number of volunteers gave of themselves holding, handling and loving these babies and with this treatment, they returned to health once again.

Everyone who has been in love knows how nurturing touch is for one's health and happiness. Just holding the loved ones hands does all kinds of things for a person. The very intimacy of that kind of feeling is not only a happy experience but likewise is calming and healing in nature. That loving touch can overcome the pain of harsh words expressed as the pressures of life close in on those in families. God has given us the gentle touch to heal not only the physical wounds but mental and emotional hurts as well. The fast and rough *macho male* approach to love making as often seen on the television is not the way to a woman's heart. Proper wooing takes time and calls for a great deal of consideration and tenderness - and the gentle touch.

Lewis Thomas, physician, professor and author of The Lives of a Cell said, "Touching is medicine's oldest secret, never acknowledged as the central, essential skill and always obscured by the dancing and the chanting - but always busily there, the laying on of hands.(1)

I began this chapter by saying that everyone has a healing touch. Your touch can heal and does heal. However, there are degrees of healing. Some seem to get better results than others and appear to have a special gift. Most of us can write, though few qualify as journalists and fewer still achieve the greatness of a Hemingway or a Shakespeare. Though there are differences in talents there are ways to improve on our basic gifts. I believe that God gave us all of us the magic of touch as a natural gift. When this gift is coupled with faith it yields far greater results. I believe that when a person shows mercy through love and caring and reaches out to comfort another, God honors his/her intentions and heals. That has been experienced even apart from religious belief, as persons of good will have reached out to help others in need. A good example of this is the loving mother, seeking to bring her child back to health by doing those things which come natural to her... hugging, holding, stroking, loving, which in themselves are nurturing and healing.

Joseph Chilton Pearce, in his book, Magical Child, tells of the marvelous effect touching has on a new-born child's rapid growth and development and speaks of the ideal way a baby should be stimulated immediately following birth. "The mother begins a slow, gentle massage that will continue off and on for weeks. Beginning with the infant's back, she caresses with her hands in slow, rhythmic, and very light movements, stimulating his/her entire body...." (2)

The author is convinced that in societies closer to the earth, that such constant touch with the mother allows for a strong bonding, gives the child a sense of peace and security and speeds up his/her learning processes beyond the levels we normally expect in our Western cultures. Pearce stresses the importance of the parent's touch to the child. He is against those things in our society which discourage that contact, such as playpens, cribs and anything else which tends to isolate a child from human touch.

I remember how soothing it was for me to feel my mother's hands as she looked after me when I was sick, as a child. Sometimes when I was feverish she would relieve the fever with a wet wash cloth on my cheeks and forehead, which made me feel so good. I can still recall her fingers going through my hair and the touch of her hands on my head. It was a healing touch ! She did not think of it as a healing touch. She was just being a mother, expressing her love and caring for her child in the way she knew best - through the touch of her hands. Haven't most of us done that very thing to someone we loved?

In primitive cultures babies are carried everywhere by their mothers, either in a pouch on the back or on the front. In the Eskimo society the baby is on his/her mother's back - sometimes underneath the parka and sometimes on the outside. I think it is a good thing that we have adapted that practice for our own. It is now an in thing to have moms and dads carrying babies attached to themselves, either on front or on the back. Perhaps being held in front of the parent is best in the beginning, but as the child grows older he/she receives some real advantages from being on the back. From that viewpoint there is the sense of being a part of their father or mother, actually feeling themselves as a participant in all that the parent is doing.

Contact sports are common to the young among all animal species and among all human cultures. There is a lot of touch involved in play. Not unlike puppies, children love to be involved in contact sports. Through the growing years we touch in our games - we play "tag", we wrestle, we tackle, we dance. We hold hands beginning with "ring around the rosie" and continue holding hands through early romance and hopefully we maintain this practice all our lives into the "golden years". Play has proven to be a stimulant to learning, beginning in primitive cultures and has been highly effective in the learning of languages. A child can learn another language with great speed when allowed to play with children of another culture. How much touch contributes to that learning process I do not know, but it's part in bonding is significant at the beginning of our lives. That is a time when we rely on our intuitive processes for almost everything. We are in fully in touch with our inner resources. When my twin daughters were still infants their mother and I use to lie on the floor with them and hug and tickle them and they squealed in glee. It was the beginning of a bonding which continues today now that they are parents and grandparents themselves.

Today we are hearing about the two brains we have within our big brain. The right brain deals with the creative, imaginative, processes, which are natural to us at birth. However, because of the emphasis in our educational systems, as children, we are led to use our left brain, which deals with logic and order. In time, most of us, particularly the men, stop using the right brain, with all of its rich potential. Our natural, intuitive ideas soon get squelched as "off the wall" and impractical. By the time our school teachers and parents have "straightened us out", we have abandoned our right brain functions. In general, women continue to use both brain functions. That is where those sarcastic remarks about "women's intuition" came into being. Fortunately, we can resurrect the right brain function once we know how important it is to us. We can get in touch with this resource by going within.

"Seeing is believing," we often hear expressed. Yet we have been told, "Blessed are those who have not seen and yet believed" . It is necessary for us to go within and get in touch with our own inner spirit if we expect to get the most from our potential. The unconscious mind in each of us is not only a vast storehouse of information but also is the source of our direction from on high. Yet, most of the time we live in the world of our conscious minds alone, where we tend to put too much reliance on what the world says - often missing the obvious, simple answers which come from our inner resources.

The magic of touch is not so much what we do to make it work - - rather it is our willingness to let go and let it happen that produces results. It is not by gritting our teeth and ordering it to happen that makes touch magic, but it is when we turn in and go with the flow that things begin to happen. As we tune in to the heartbeat of the universe we can know peace, we can know love, we can know joy. It is not through some rigid system of keeping the law that we are able to be made whole, but by simply allowing the gift of God's grace to come through to us and to others.

We can do it spiritually, not with the kind of prayer that gives instructions nor the kind that preaches a sermon to the one in need, but with thoughts where we tune in and let the inner voice take over. As I said at the beginning of this chapter, touch is important to us. It plays an important part in the bonding we have with our parents at the beginning of our lives. It creates within us a good feeling in ourselves and allows us to trust the intuitive side of our natures within. Touch becomes a magic touch when we use the same procedure of prayerfully tuning in and reaching out to someone in a caring way. Then our touch will be nourishing to that person. It can bring to them peace and love and joy. It can lift another's spirit. It can set another free. The magic of touch can heal the sick.

Chapter 2

Getting in Touch

The secret to finding our potential in life is learning how to get in touch with the source of all wisdom. Jesus knew that secret all his life. He was in touch with the Christ spirit within. He knew that God was his true father and he had the ability to get in touch with him. At the age of twelve he upset his earthly parents, Joseph and Mary by taking off for the temple to visit with the teachers and scholars, who were greatly impressed with him. When his parents found him, he was surprised that they did not understand that it was natural for him to be there. "Did you not know that I was bound to be in my Father's house? He told us that the way to get in touch with the Father is to seek first the Kingdom of God, that is, to find the Christ spirit within ourselves. There we shall find the answer to the meaning of life . We seek the Kingdom by going inside, to the depths of our unconscious minds and beyond. The Kingdom of Heaven is within us.

We are often unaware of the resources available to us from within because our conscious minds command our attention most of the time. However, it is on the level of the unconscious that the Eternal becomes known to us. His spirit communicates with our spirit within. Unless we are in the habit of tuning in, much of the inspiration he provides for us never reaches our conscious thought. We complain that he is not available, that he has deserted us, when in reality he is there at all times. He is ready to speak to us, ready to lead us, ready to enable us with power. He is as close to us as our own unconscious minds. The move is ours. It is up to us to open the door and let him in.

Our intuitive resources are constantly working in our behalf and much that they do for us we credit to chance or coincidence. Some people seem to be luckier, they always win the door prizes. Others are better at finding things. That has been one of my gifts through the years, the gift of just knowing where a lost item can be found.

I believe that when we begin to live, daily trusting in the guidance of our higher power, we are led to the right places, even when our conscious minds are not asking for any special request. Those who are close to me are aware that I have what people call "good luck" finding parking spaces. I do not believe that it is just good luck. Neither is it prayer, in the usual sense of that word. It is when I am in touch with my inner self, the "self" that is always in touch with the source of all wisdom. So without making a specific prayer request for a parking space, somehow a space is provided for me because I am in tune with my inner being. When we are in harmony with the universe our inner selves are constantly being of service to us. I know that I depend on my intuitive guide when I am looking for a gift for someone special. I'll enter a gift store and a clerk will ask, "Can I help you find something ?" and I always answer, "I'm not sure what I'm looking for, but when I find it I'll know that it's the right thing." How true that is, for when I do see the gift item it will be better than anything else that I had thought of before. Somehow my inner guide knew that the perfect gift was in that store. All I had to do was to look over the place carefully in order to find it.

"Living in the Spirit" is an accurate description of

that style of life. We are prepared at all times to receive direction for our lives. The many success stories of Alcoholics Anonymous demonstrate how giving up our personal control to enable Him to control is really what works. Step Three of the AA Program states, "Made a decision to turn our will and our lives over to the care of God as we understand him". That is what I am talking about when I say "going within". Our conscious minds want to be in control. Our Egos are threatened when we put our trust in the intuitive and spiritual parts of our being. But when we do, things happen. Following are some examples of tuning in and making use of your right brain - or letting go and allowing it to happen.

My wife and I had gone to an outdoor concert held in a large grassy area during the summer. There was plenty of light at eight o'clock when the concert began but the night was black when we got up to leave. We walked in a sea of people through the darkness towards the parking lot when I reached in my pocket and noticed that my recent birthday present from Jo, a cigarette lighter, was missing. Thinking only of retrieving that lost item I said, "Wait here and I'll be right back." If I had stopped to think about it I would have reasoned, "If I dropped it where we were sitting I could never find the spot now among all these people and in this darkness." Fortunately for me, I did not stop to think about it. In great haste I worked my way against the surging tide of people, and continued until I arrived at a certain place, reached down and without looking, I grasped the lighter in my hand. I stood up, put it in my pocket and ran back to the place where my wife had been waiting. It wasn't until later that I became aware of the unusual thing that had occurred. How did I know the exact spot where I had dropped the lighter and how did my hands find it in the dark? Years ago someone might have said that I found it with my "sixth sense". Others might call it ESP or extra sensory perception. Now I know that I had received help from my spirit within, from my intuitive guide.

I can think of two other instances where I received that kind of help. On one occasion I had lost my watch while tossing a football with my son at our cabin. I didn't discover the loss until the next day. By the time I got back to our vacation spot, the ground was entirely covered with leaves. Searching for a watch seemed hopeless. In my need I turned to my guardian angel and said, " I'll never find the watch without your help. Please take me to it". I sat there for a while waiting for some direction. Then I picked up a rake and walked until my legs came to a standstill. I moved the rake towards the leaves in front of me and picked off the top leaves. As the leaves were removed I saw a bright spot of gold shining up at me. It was my watch ! In that large area covered with leaves I had moved to the exact spot and found the watch on my first attempt.

Another incident was similar. In a snowstorm, I had lost my only key to a neighbor's house which was in my care. I was not aware of the loss until I had returned home after making a check on the premises. When I went out to my car it had begun to snow. As I approached the house I could see that the driveway and sidewalk were covered with about an inch of snow, certainly enough to conceal a single key. Remembering my previous experience, I went through the same procedure. I had a small shovel in my hand and after I received my direction and came to what I thought was the place to dig, I dug in and brought up nothing but snow. I stopped immediately and tuned in again. I began to shovel again...slowly, slowly, with great care. Then, without even touching its surface I saw it in front of me. Even though it was in the darkness of night, the metal surface of the key was reflecting the glow of a streetlight in the distance. In both of these cases, it would have been an impossible job to find the exact location of these objects with conscious reasoning alone. There was too much area to cover and the leaves in one place, and the snow in the other, had completely covered the ground. Yet, with a prayer and the willingness to trust direction from within, I was able to go to the precise spots where the objects were to be found.

On my way back from a conference I had a layover on a Saturday in Washington, D.C. At that time, I knew that my grandson was there with a group of students. I had no address and no phone number for him. Yet, something kept saying to me, "Maybe you'll run into Kent while you're here". I went about the day like any tourist, making a visit to old Alexandria and finally ended up in a restaurant for dinner. Though there were many to choose from, one of them seemed just right... and I knew why when my grandson, Kent, came up the stairs past my table. Coincidence is what some may call it, but to me that was evidence of the eternal guidance of the Spirit within.

After I had shared these experiences with my friend, Don Langworthy, he said, "I believe you...listen to what happened to me. I dropped my ring in a huge empty parking lot which was covered with snow which had melted and become ice. It was getting dark. After continual searching, with no good results I kicked blindly at the ice expressing my frustration and up popped my ring which was lifted out of the ice by the force of my kick." Perhaps you can think of something similar that happened to you?

These gifts continue to occur throughout our lives. We are here to claim our portion of the *abundant life,* but to claim it we must be daring enough to do those things we *feel* we should do. We cannot expect to have all the answers before we launch out on a new program. We have to learn to trust in God's guidance as it is expressed through our intuitive wisdom. When I was serving as the Vicar of St. Matthias Church in Seaside, California, I drove past the place where they were building a new city hall and received a picture of myself being installed as a city councilman. How could that be if I had no plan to enter politics? A few months later I had an "aha" experience when the mayor came to my house to ask if I would accept his appointment to fill the vacancy that had occurred on the council. Once we become tuned in to our inner resources, we receive assurances like that all the time. We begin to dare to trust in his guidance. That is when our imagination and creativity come into play. Throughout history a few brave souls dared to trust their dreams, dared to press forward in spite of the ridicule of others and in the process made life more beautiful for the human race.

Jesus challenged a few rough-cut individuals, who took his message to the world and the value of human life was changed forever. He dared to say that each one of us is of intrinsic value and stood behind his words when he gave his life for us. From that time until today the free nations of the world have defended the rights of individuals. Those who have heard his voice have made

24

his stand the battle cry for freedom and justice for all races, creeds, tongues...for the oppressed, whether they are men, women or children and even for the unborn.

Columbus was thought to be a fool, insisting that the world was round, but he prevailed and eventually found a new continent. Louis Pasteur was ridiculed for his theories in the field of bacteriology, but see how blessed we are today, free from so many diseases which plagued mankind for years. The Wright brothers had a dream about making a craft that would fly and we now travel all over the world in a matter of hours. These were people who could go within and come up with a new idea, something they could see in their mind's eye...but then, they had the determination to bring it to life.

We have received similar blessings from the efforts of artists, composers, explorers and great statesmen...those who dared to dream and to follow the guiding light from within. At the present time too much reliance is being put in the hands of unimaginative, unfeeling persons, who have the power to bring destruction upon the world. I mentioned earlier that too many men have abandoned their creative right-brained functions in favor of the less sensitive left-brained functions. Most of those who are in high places in the military in the world are left-brain thinkers. When they think of strategy they use charts and plans showing targets as geographical sites. Faces of actual human beings never get into the picture. The human factor is missing. In a closed room full of impersonal objects, such as maps and diagrams, these logical people merely estimate the position of missiles and the amount of fire power to effect a successful strike on an enemy position. They never stop to consider that innocent people will be killed or maimed in such an attack. We need to get more intuitive, feeling people in places of authority, in order to change the self-destruct course we are following. We need to move from negative thinking to positive thinking, from impersonal logic to personal concern for human life.

The potential is there. We all have it. Even those who have shut off their right-brain functions can reclaim those abilities. It will take some effort and time, but just opening our minds to the possibility will allow it to begin. The more we use our intuitive abilities, the more successful we become. When we begin to walk "in the spirit", our hearts are lighter, our energy levels increase and our minds become open to all sorts of possibilities. We increase our creative endeavors and we can hardly keep up with all the good ideas that come our way.

Without knowing it, you have been using your intuitive resources for years. Just reading about some of my experiences may bring to light some of the times when you were led to do just the right thing. However, once you have become aware of that powerhouse within you, you can increase your abilities on this level. You will begin to trust the suggestions which come to your mind and will dare to do what you formerly were afraid to do.

There was a time in the history of mankind when we human beings had a greater sensory awareness than we do now. Most animals have a heightened sense of smell...are even tuned in to earthquakes...before they begin. The animals seem to be able to sense the presence of danger. We have lost most of those gifts by lack of use. We have ignored our intuitive natures so long that we have almost lost those abilities as well.

Those intuitive ways are still with us. We just do not pay any attention to how they are working in our lives. Have you ever noticed how your fingers will have already picked out the right key from your key chain when you reach into your pants pocket or your purse? Somehow your fingers see and feel which one is needed.

Have you ever watched a natural athlete catch a baseball while running away from it? At a certain point, without turning around to look, he reaches up into the air and "backhands it" into his glove. How does he know where to reach for it...when to do so ? Certainly, practice and knowledge of the game play a part, but the real direction comes from within. He is following his intuitive leanings and the time to reach for the ball is almost an automatic move. The ballplayer is trusting to his inner sense of direction. He may not even know that he is, but that is what he is doing. He has done it before and it has worked and the more he continues to trust his intuitive side, the more it will continue to work in his life.

That is how prayer works. Many of our learned prayers are beautiful thoughts, but are essentially teaching tools. Unless we are saying them with faith and expectancy they are little more than lip service. The kind of prayers I am referring to are those which are written for general usage. These prayers can still work, because our higher power understands our needs and answers us even when the words are not right for the occasion. He/She responds when we reach out in faith and trust. Our spiritual guide speaks to our unconscious mind and often we are not aware of any voice or influence on our decisions. When we relax and submit our lives to God in simple trust, then we shall receive help.

It is time for us to start paying attention to our inner

voice, which is the key to the kingdom of heaven. The kingdom is within us. Going within is the key to knowing ourselves better...it unlocks the door to those things that are most important in life. It is the way to get the most out of our minds...and best of all, it is the access to that higher power we know as God. If tuning in is such a great thing, how do we do it? How do we receive these inner messages? The first thing we have to do is to remove the distractions of our conscious world. Seek out a quiet space, free from TV and the radio. We really do not need background music or or any other sounds that could be distracting. We just need to be quiet, slow down, relax and give our minds a rest. Lay aside your musts and shoulds for a while. Forget about what you are going to prepare for supper. You are there to receive thoughts and inspirations, so stop keeping your mind so busy. Your Ego is afraid of having you go within, so you may have to make a conscious effort to stop thinking. Your conscious mind may want to lay out a plan for tomorrow, but your inner spirit may come up with a new plan for life.

It is easier to get in touch than you think. You can be at your desk with lots of work to do and still find a time to be quiet and tune in. The more we practice tuning in, the easier it becomes for us. The intuitive resource is always available to us when we must make decisions. Many times we may get an idea, but because it seems so off the all, we discard it for something more acceptable, more practical.

The intuitive messages are always right for us, but the problem is that we do not always read them correctly. As a result when we begin to use the method of going within we shall make some mistakes. This is the old trial and error method, as we often

28

learn what to do, by doing it wrong. However, in time we become more adept at understanding the messages we are receiving from our own intuition, which in turn may be messages from an angel guide or possibly the Holy Spirit.

Chapter 3

The Healing Touch

We have seen how important touch is for our life and health. I have said that it is nourishing, that it excites us and makes us feel good, that under certain circumstances that touch can be a healing touch.

From primitive times there have been healers of one sort or another. Most of them have used some kind of touch as they attempted to heal the sick. In ancient times, sickness was always thought to be inflicted on people by evil spirits. The healer's task was to drive away the evil spirits by incantations or dances. Sometimes, they tried to drive them out of the patient's body by beating the sick person.

Early on, the medicine person also began to learn about certain plants and herbs which were helpful to people when they were ill. Recent studies have revealed that some very profound discoveries were made by them. Some of them were apparently good psychologists and counselors, quite unlike the depictions of witch doctors that we see in the movies. While they acted according to their superstitions and traditions, they also began to use medications which were beneficial to the sick.

In Western civilization and the Orient, physicians have been practicing medicine for centuries. "Practicing" is a good word because doctors admit that they do not know all the answers. In our time, great advances have been made in surgery, immunization, and pharmacology. When antibiotics were discovered in the thirties, it was believed that they could cure almost anything. Now that we have lived with them for a few decades, we realize their many limitations. We continue to be challenged by such old bugaboos as cancer and heart disease as well as new illnesses that appear. Today, AIDS has become the present unsolved dilemma for the medical world. Most physicians will readily admit that there is much more to healing people than surgery and medicines. We often hear the words "holistic medicine" as an attempt to describe the many dimensions of healing - physical, mental, emotional and spiritual.

In my experience, most holistic seminars that are held do not involve on the one hand, many medical doctors, or on the other hand, people in religious healing ministries. You see everything there from health food experts promoting diet and exercise to those doing reflexology, hypnotism or acupuncture. Most of those at holistic conferences do their healing through using their natural healing gifts and/or through mental thought processes. Often, they do achieve good results, as in secular therapeutic touch, but they must rely on their own talents and abilities. As a Christian minister, I have used prayer and the healing touch, looking to God as the one providing the healing. Glen Clark spoke to this in his book, I Will Lift Up Mine Eyes, when he described one method as the John the Baptist method, by the law and the other as the Jesus way, by grace.

"The method of John, where strong men would take the Kingdom of Heaven by force, is where the person who prays, concentrates his thoughts upon the friend he would help, and by strength of thought forces the trouble to leave. The method of Jesus, on the other hand, ignores the trouble and sees only the Father and His Kingdom...This entails no work, for the Father, not we, does the work; whereas the other method requires an immense amount of work"[1]

At the beginning of my ministry in the Church, I found out that God was using me as an instrument of his healing. I merely prayed for people, using compassion and sincerity, and they were healed - not because of my knowledge, but by the grace of God. As time went on I learned more about the ministry of healing and also developed whatever natural gifts I possessed, but my approach still is the Jesus Way. Sometimes, it has taken only a touch to do the job. The following tells of my experience on one of my hospital visits.

My friend, Rod, lay face down on the hospital bed. He had just had surgery on the disks of his spine. He was in great distress. "Let's see if we can relieve the pain, "I said. "Show me where it hurts the most". "Right here," he said, lifting his hand behind his back and pointing with his index finger to the middle of his spine, "Careful, it sure is sensitive."

Moving closer to his bed, I held my hand over the sore spot and then very gently touched the wounded area with my fingers. "That's it !" he said. "The pain is gone!". I thought, "Why, I haven't even begun my prayer". Still not accepting what had happened, I questioned him again, "Are you sure the pain has gone"? "Sure I'm sure," he replied. "It stopped the moment you touched me."

I was surprised at the swiftness of the healing action.

I really did not have the time to say a prayer. Yet that was my intention - to bring about relief through the laying on of hands with prayer. I was in the proper attitude for healing and so was the patient, who believed that I possessed healing gifts. My prayerful intention and a simple touch was all that was needed to take away his pain. You see, I didn't do the healing. God did...the Jesus way. I just followed the direction of the voice within. The easing of pain was a gift of grace. Complete healing was to take a lot longer. Rod had to be careful following the surgery to take good care of his body through eating the right food and doing the proper exercises. In time he was restored to good health again.

There have been many other instances of healing by a single touch in my ministry. However, in most cases spiritual healing takes time, as is the case in medical healing. However, once one experiences healing by a touch, he knows it is always a possibility. I believe in the magic of touch as a gift God handed to human beings at the time of our creation. Through using that gift we have been able to energize others who were weak, express our love and caring and bring the sick back to a state of health again. Since the dawn of, civilization there have been healers who have achieved some degree of success, using their God-given talents and common sense. We still have all that going for us, and then some, when we bring Christ into the picture. After becoming acquainted with Jesus, we who believe in him have been able to use these natural gifts of touch in his service. He enables us to do better by giving us the "Gifts of the Spirit" as additional resources. We offer his healing touch to others and often get the same good results that he did.

I first began using the healing touch with my twin daughters. When they were babies laying my hands on them for healing came natural to me. It was easy for me to learn with my own children, who trusted me and looked to Daddy for help, I felt no embarrassment as I might have if I had been dealing with adults. Though I knew very little about spiritual healing, which relies on faith and intuitive guidance, my primary concern was the relief of my sick children. As the son of a physician and a nurse, I did not hesitate to bind their wounds and sooth them by touching them gently with my hands with good results. As I laid hands on them I prayed to God to help me bring about the desired result. Often the result was exactly what I prayed for. I continued these practices throughout their childhood and in time I became more proficient and expanded the practice beyond my family to any who came to me in need.

It did not take Linda and Donna long to imitate my healing practices. Starting with dolls, they soon moved to the animals in our home. Hamsters are very responsive to warm and loving hands. Often these pets will become cold and appear to be dead and may die if not attended to. Donna first discovered that her pet hamster could revive if she were held and stroked lovingly and given bodily warmth. To see "Mother Hamster" come alive had all the appearance of a true resurrection. Being able to heal these animals gave my daughters a confidence and an ability to look after the needs of others, that they have never lost.

Years later, as mothers, they have been able to function as healers with their families and friends. Having experienced the touch of healing hands so early in their lives, my children were able to trust their intuitive directions in the area of healing. When sick, they always called upon me to use prayer and healing touch. Even when I have offered them antihistamines or "Turns", they have preferred my spiritual ministrations. Years later Donna told me that it even worked for tooth aches. She said that if she told me she had a tooth ache I would send her to the dentist, which she hated. So instead, she used to tell me that she had a pain in her head... and I would pray for that, and it would relieve the tooth ache. Of course, our teeth are in our head, aren't they? As young women they were also ready to offer those ministrations to others.

As young women, involved with their husbands in a bowling league, they found an opportunity to come to the help of a spectator they found in distress. The mother of the bowlers was feeling a great deal of pain. They quickly went to her assistance and offered their healing touch. It takes some courage to do that sort of thing in a secular setting. A bowling alley may seem out of context for something like healing prayer...but where does the need present itself... in a medical center or in church, or in the arena of life ? Jesus did all of his healing out in the world. In this instance, Linda and Donna were able to relieve the woman's pain until she could be seen by her physician.

On one occasion they came to my rescue while we were all engaged in building a summer cabin for Linda and her husband, Larry. Actually, Larry was the builder and I was his unskilled assistant, who slipped and sprained an ankle. By evening the ankle was swollen severely and I was unable to put my weight on it. They used a method described elsewhere in this book, called the Therapeutic Touch, which Linda had learned as a nurse and shared with the rest of us. Each one took turns moving their hands over and around the injured ankle that evening. After they had done this for a while the pain left me, though the ankle was still swollen. However, in the morning when I arose the swelling had left completely and I was able to put both shoes on. Once I dared to step on it I found out that indeed, I had been healed. And who were the healers ? Donna and Linda, my own children, now grown and ministering to me.

Now that their children are almost all out of the nest, Donna and Linda are still involved with healing touch. Linda has her degree in nursing and has worked as a school nurse and worked in obstetrics, often comforting women in labor and being among the first to handle infants right after they are born. There were many times when she saw the need to use the Therapeutic Touch to assist in the healing process and was happy to have that additional skill. Now she is a Public Health nurse dealing with pregnant teenagers where compassion is one of her main tools.

Donnas' healing hands were used often in massaging her family members through the years. After the children were grown she made a serious study of massage and finally became a licensed masseuse. She now has a practice where she uses the accepted massage techniques, but also offers her healing touch, using crystals and chakra balancing, not my system, but getting positive results, following her intuitive guidance and faith. She deals with more than their physical needs but their hopes and dreams and attitudes as well.

Touch continues to play a significant part in their lives and I am thankful that my early and frequent use of touch with them may have helped them to be more

36

sensitive to the many dimensions of touch. As I did with my daughters, I introduced my son, Philip, to the world of touch as soon as he arrived home from the hospital. My primary means of relieving his pain or healing his hurts was the healing touch. I never instructed him in doing this for others, but very early in his life, he knew that he too could offer healing to another. First it was demonstrated when I was suffering from an injury.

I had injured my shoulder and it was hurting quite a bit when I joined him in his bed to read a story. He could see my obvious distress as I cut the story short and turned over, hoping to relieve the pain. As I lay there suffering with the hurt shoulder, I felt a small hand touch me on that spot. No words were exchanged...just the touch. It was a "healing touch". The next day I was in good shape again because my child cared enough for me to trust his intuitive self and take an action that would lead to healing. Dad was hurting and needed help so Phil did what came to him naturally - he offered a healing touch. Of course, he had also learned by example and he had practiced the role of healer in play. However, it still took trust in his inner direction to act in a real life situation. My grown daughters, mentioned previously, are skilled at giving the "healing touch" because as children, they too were not ashamed to trust their inner direction and act upon it.

When Phil was about six years old, I let him help me as an acolyte for the mid-week service in our church. We had rehearsed the task of the server... when to bring the bread and when to bring the water and wine, but he was still a bit nervous doing the real thing at a service. It has been my practice at those midweek Eucharist's to offer the "Laying on of hands" for those desiring healing. At this particular service, when I placed my hand on the head of one who had come forward, I was surprised to find Phil's hand there as well. Though he was worried about the learned functions of a server, he was confident of his intuitive functions as a minister of healing. In this instance he was operating on two levels. As the server for the priest, he was acting on the surface level of intelligence, those things he had been taught to do. First, bring the bread...then the cruets of water and wine...place towel on arm ...etc., etc.. He was somewhat anxious functioning on that level. However, when he joined me in the healing function he was confident of his actions, for in this instance he was in touch with his unconscious mind, where he could easily follow the guidance of the still small voice within.

I believe that the healing touch is most effective when we rely on our intuitive selves, following the direction that comes from within. It is when I have allowed the inner voice to completely dominate my thinking and my action? twit I have had the greatest success in healing others including the healing of cancers, especially one massive brain tumor where I was giving the last "rites" In the most incredible cases, those that were considered incurable, I did not even expect healing. While my conscious mind was in a state of disbelief, never-the-less, I was still able to let myself be directed from within and gave them the prayer of healing in spite of the apparent hopelessness of their situation. The still small voice knew better than I and the persons were healed, much to my surprise.

Years ago when I was attending theological school, we were warned of the dangers of touching or getting too close to others, particularly members of the opposite sex, when visiting them at home or in the hospital. The emphasis was on maintaining a proper space between you and the other person. "Keep your distance", we were told.

However, as I became a practicing minister and learned about the laying on of hands, I found out that the advantages of touch far outweighed the disadvantages. In fact, it is a common thing for a patient to offer you his/her hand when you are standing next to the bed.

Whenever this has happened to me, my natural reaction has been to accept that hand and continue to hold it until the patient wanted to release it. Of course, there is always a chance that she/he will not let you go. You may be staying there longer than you wish. When that occurs, you realize how important touch is for others. Holding your hand not only comforts those who are sick but also quiets their fears and helps them to feel secure.

In recent times we have seen a bumper sticker asking, "Have you hugged your kid today?" This reminds us of the importance of another kind of touch that nurtures our children. Actually, all of us need that kind of nurture. Today, most of the liturgical churches have revised their Eucharistic liturgy to include the kiss of peace', present in the mass in the early days of the Christian Church. When it was first introduced as a handshake, people felt awkward and often resisted this innovation. However, with the passage of time, it has become, to many, a favorite part of the service and the formal clasping of hands has often given way to enthusiastic bear hugs.

Sometimes a hug can be healing as well. I am

reminded of a story told by Matt Linn, S.J., priest and author. One Sunday, when he was feeling out of sorts with himself and the world, he attended mass in a parish where he was not known. He pulled the white insert from his clergy shirt to make himself inconspicuous and hid in one of the back pews of the church. He seemed to be safe from the intrusion of people until the Peace, when a huge woman next to him gave him such an embrace she lifted him off the floor. At that point he was so overwhelmed and amused, that he felt loved and restored. He just said, "I give up, God", and rejoined the human race by continuing to pass the peace to others.

As wonderful as hugging and touch may seem to you, it is important to remember that not everyone shares your enthusiasm on this subject. Some persons are offended by hugging, considering it to be an invasion of their privacy. Even though you may feel that a good hug would be beneficial, you must be sensitive to the feelings of all kinds of people.

A young mother came to our healing service because of depression. She felt alienated from God and people. She sat in the back of the church and remained aloof from all others. When some of our members greeted one another with warm hugs she stepped back so that no one would approach her in that manner. After a few more meetings, her attitude began to change as she shared in the conversation and the prayers. None of our members forced themselves on her for she had made it known how she felt about that type of touch. With the passage of time, she began to trust the members and to feel comfortable with our group. Finally, she stepped forth and reached out to others. Later on, when she was feeling accepted and loved and ready to face her world, she

40

laughed as she said, "Remember me when I first came here, how I didn't want anyone to touch me? Well, now I really enjoy giving hugs myself...and receiving them too!" I really believe that if our members had invaded her privacy during her early time with us that we might have lost her.

In her case, the best thing we did was to be patient and give her time to get to know us. That is not always easy for people to do. Some are so anxious to help that they press too hard. The same thing occurs with others after a conversion experience or the baptism of the Spirit. In their desire to share that great experience with others, the new converts can drive away the very ones they desire to bring to Jesus. We can achieve much greater success by being sensitive and caring and giving others the time they need to feel comfortable.

The touch that brings healing is a delightful surprise. Duane approached me with smiles all over and said, "It really works! The moment your hands touched the sore spot on my back, the pain left...just like that". At our midweek noonday Eucharist we offer prayers for healing. Duane had come to that service unaware of that practice, and he just happened to have a backache. When I invited the people to receive the laying on of hands, he came along as well. One touch and he was healed.

It would be nice if all healings came so easily. In my experience healings by a single touch come few and far between. As a result, we use a number of different methods in ministering to the sick. Perhaps the laying on of hands in the most common because it is so natural for us to do when we wish to comfort someone. As parents we hold our children when they are hurting or sick and we lovingly caress them, stroking their heads and backs as we gently assure them that "everything's going to be all right".

Even the kiss which takes away the pain from the weeping child is a kind of healing touch, a healing prayer reduced to the well known, "let Mommy kiss it". Simple as it is, it has all the ingredients necessary for healing of any kind. It starts out with a need. Someone is hurting. Secondly, there is faith, faith that another person can help. Then there is expectation. When her mother is found, the child believes that the pain will stop when she kisses it. It also takes the action of another person, someone who is willing to move out as a minister of healing - in this case, the child's mother.

You can see how that can be applied to a situation which involves you and a sick person. The one hurting is also a little child inside who has a real need. Her parents are not there, but you are and if you respond in the right way... if you show that you care and then act with authority, you can enable the one who is sick to have faith in your treatment. The patient will have some expectancy of results from your prayers. That brings us to the next ingredient, your faith. When the patient's faith is lacking, it is your faith which must come to the fore. That gives you the authority needed to serve as God's healer.

You know that prayer and a loving touch can heal, just as a mother knows that her kiss will soothe her child. When you act with authority and are truly caring, and truly believing, the sick person will receive a healing touch. He may not be totally healed, but he will know that he has received a treatment that made him feel better inside and gave him hope for the future. If he

42

was in pain there is a good chance that the pain has eased or left entirely - in the same way that the pain leaves the little child when her mother heals her with a kiss.

Chapter 4

The Jesus Touch

To be touched by Jesus was to be healed.

When he saw Peter's mother-in-law, "He touched her hand" and the fever left her (Matt 8:14 RSV).

Then there was the time with the two blind men who came to him for healing and he "touched their eyes...and their eyes were opened" (Matt 9:29 RSV).

The touch seemed to work both ways. If Jesus couldn't get to them, they were determined to reach out to him. We all have heard of the woman who had a hemorrhage for twelve years, who cried out in desperation, "If I can only touch his cloak, I shall be cured" (Matt 9: 21 NEB). And we also know the rest of the story, that she was indeed healed instantly.

In the Gospel of Mark we read that "all who had diseases pressed upon him to 'touch him" (Mark 3:10 RSV), and further on in Mark's account we find that "all who touched him were cured" (Mark 6:5 NEB).

What was that remarkable quality in the Jesus touch that healed people instantly ? Most of the time, those of us in healing take minutes, hours, days and even years to bring about a cure - and sometimes never do achieve our goal. That goes for doctors as well as those in the practice of spiritual healing. Yet, Jesus could merely touch the sick and they would be made whole.

As I said at the beginning of Chapter 2, Jesus knew how to get to the source of power. He identified completely with God the Father. He loved his heavenly Father dearly and even referred to him affectionately as Abba Father or Daddy. He also made it clear that the Father was the one who was doing the good works. That oneness with God was the key to his healing power and he offered us the same opportunity to perform as he did. In order to accomplish that, we must have faith in him. As he became one with the Father, so we must become one with him. "Do you not believe that I am in the Father, and the Father in me? I am not myself the source of the words I speak to you: it is the Father who dwells in me doing his own work. Believe me when I say that I am in the Father and the Father in me; or else accept the evidence of the deeds themselves. In truth, in very truth I tell you, he who has faith in me will do what I am doing; and he will do greater things still because I am going to the Father" (John 14:10-13).

In other words, Jesus was saying that he could heal because he had a direct line to the Father and that we could likewise heal by keeping in touch with him daily on our own direct line. It did not take long for his followers to experience the proof of his promise to them. In the "Acts of the Apostles", we read that, after Jesus had departed and the Holy Spirit has fallen on them, that they were able to do the special things that he had done.

"They met constantly to hear the apostles teach, and to share the common life, to break bread, and to pray. A sense of awe was everywhere, and many marvels and signs were brought about through the apostles" (Acts 2:4244 NEB).

45

On their way to the temple, Peter and John came upon a man who had been lame from birth. His friends carried him daily to the gates of the temple, so that he could beg from the people who were going inside.

"When he saw Peter and John on their way into the temple he asked for charity. But Peter fixed his eyes on him, as John did also, and said, 'Look at us.' Expecting a gift from them, the man was all attention. And Peter said, 'I have no silver or gold; but what I have I give you: in the name of Jesus Christ of Nazareth, walk.' Then he grasped him by the right hand and pulled him up; and at once his feet and ankles grew strong; he sprang up, stood on his feet, and started to walk. He entered the temple with them, leaping and praising God as he went. Everyone saw him walking and praising God, and when they recognized him as the man who used to sit begging at Beautiful Gate, they were filled with wonder and amazement at what had happened to him " (Acts 3: 1-10 NEB).

That was another case of a laying on of hands with the healing coming at once. As he took the lame man by the hand, healing energy entered into his legs immediately. Just as Jesus had said, the apostles now were the ones who were using the healing touch. As that information made its way back to the others of the twelve, I am sure that they remembered what he said, " He who has faith in me will do as I am doing".

One common thread woven into all the healings of Jesus was his method of viewing each individual case as unique. The way he dealt with each person was geared to that person's needs. He often made remarks about the faith of those requesting prayer.

"A blind man, sitting along the side of the road near

Jericho, cried out to him. "Jesus stopped and ordered the man to be brought to him, 'What do you want me to do for you?" "Sir, I want my sight back', he answered. Jesus said to him, ' Have back your sight; your faith has cured you.' He recovered his sight instantly and he followed Jesus, praising God" (Luke 18: 40-43 NEB).

In some cases, it appeared that Jesus had more than one purpose when he healed the sick. There were times when he wanted the healing to state a case for his own authority. In the following example he had three things in mind: the patient's inner spiritual need first, followed later by his physical need and thirdly it gave him opportunity to show that his authority came from on high. That was the story of the man who was paralyzed, who was taken on a litter to the house where Jesus was teaching a group of people who had gathered there, some friendly and some who were challenging his authority. There was such congestion in that place that the friends of the sick man hauled him up onto the patio roof, lowering him down, bed and all, in the midst of the crowd, right where Jesus was standing.

Now to look at the man, one would say that his primary need was obvious. He was paralyzed! However, Jesus did not even mention the patient's paralyzed state. You can imagine what his friends thought when they heard Jesus' words, which indicated his feelings that the paralytic's greatest need was spiritual.

When Jesus saw their faith, he said, 'Man, your sins are forgiven you.' The lawyers and the Pharisees began saying to themselves, 'Who is this fellow with the blasphemous talk? Who but God alone can forgive

47

sins?' But Jesus knew what they were thinking and answered them: 'Why do you harbor thoughts like these? Is it easier to say, "Your sins are forgiven you", or to say, "Stand up and walk"? But to convince you that the Son of Man has the right on earth to forgive sins' - he turned to the paralyzed man - 'I say to you, stand up, take your bed, and go home.' And at once he rose to his feet before their eyes, took up the bed he had been lying on, and went home praising God. They were all lost in amazement and praised God; filled with awe they said, 'You would never believe the things we have seen today.'"(Luke 5: 20-26 NEB).

Now some healings, which appeared to be strictly physical in nature may well have dealt with a mental or spiritual need. In his book, Creation Continues, the Jungian psychiatrist, Fritz Kunkel, gave an interesting interpretation to the first passage I cited in this chapter, the healing of Peter's mother-in-law. Knowing the probable difficult circumstances of Peter's household since he had left his family to follow Jesus, Kunkel believed that there was a good case for resentment on the part of this woman, in bed with a fever.[1]

As she lay there in bed, she might have been thinking some of these thoughts. "Everything had been fine with us so long as Peter was there, doing his fishing and looking after the needs of the family. But now, ever since he met that rabbi, Jesus, Peter has lost his senses," so she may have thought. It was a good Jew's responsibility to look after his mother-in-law and not go charging off after some itinerant preacher. "And now, to add insult to injury, he is bringing him here and if he expects me to cook and wait on that Jesus...well, I'm not about to do anything of the kind!" According to the customs of her society, she really could not refuse to be

48

a hostess when he came to their home. But, she may have found another way. She became ill.

Now, I'm not suggesting that she did this on purpose. Whenever we develop a psycho-somatic illness we are totally unaware of it, for we are, indeed, sick. If it is a headache, your head really hurts. If is a heart attack, your life is really in danger. Only the cause is mental. The rest of it is real. So Peter's mother-in-law really was sick and in bed when Jesus arrived. In fact, her fever may well have been due to a virus, alone. Even so, Fritz Kunkel's theory does make sense to me, for he contended that when the sick lady was brought face to face with Jesus, something happened to her within her heart and soul. When she could look into the eyes of Jesus and see all the love and compassion there, any resentments she may have had concerning him vanished. Her only desire now was to serve him. Jesus knew that it was a hardship for the families of the men who left home to follow him. When the wives, brothers, sisters and children of the disciples came to know him, they too loved him and understood why it was necessary for their loved one to leave home.

In all physical healings there is some corresponding mental or spiritual need. When Jesus met and prayed with her and held her hand, "the fever left her" and any of the resentments she may have had, left her as well. For the Bible account goes on to say, "and she got up and waited on him"(Matthew 8:15).

Jesus was a master at looking at a person and knowing what was going on inside of that person. We read earlier how he looked past the paralyzed body of the man on the litter to a soul bound by the chains of his own guilt. Jesus forgave him and broke those chains, making it possible for him to be freed from the paralysis which bound his body.

He met the Samaritan woman at the well and he, a Jew, gave her status by speaking to her and then revealed to her how he knew the inner secrets of her mind, of her loose moral life. At the same time he showed her his unconditional love as he offered her the gift of the waters of eternal life.

Once when he was teaching in a synagogue he noticed a woman, bent double in the congregation (Luke: 11-13). The New English Bible translation says that she was "possessed by a spirit that had crippled her for eighteen years". The J.B. Phillips translation says that "she had been ill from some psychological cause". Jesus told her that she was free from her illness and when he put his hand on her she stood upright immediately.

I wonder if Jesus had seen her previously and knew of her psychological or spiritual needs. Perhaps, in her case too, it was a matter of his being able to reach into her unconscious mind and know what was needed. Sometimes when we are confronted with a sick person, we too receive a word of knowledge, which speaks to us of the real problem within. Most frequently when we come face to face with psychological problems, we need some time with the sick person. I remember one time during a healing service, having a woman come forward for the "healing of memories". I laid hands on her with prayer and she stood up, full of joy and cried out, "I'm healed, thank God - I feel just great!" To the people in the church it must have seemed like the "bent over woman", one touch and she was healed. It really wasn't that simple. The congregation did not know that during the previous day I had spent more than an hour with her privately, praying for her and discussing with her some of her problems, which had paved the way for the healing that was to come in the church that night.

Occasionally, we are asked to pray for people over the phone, sometimes calling from great distances. Very often we feel that those prayers are effective - people are healed. We also have intercessory prayer at healing services and pray alone for those who may be miles away. Jesus showed more than once that prayer could heal from a distance. Perhaps the best known of these healings is the story of the Centurion's servant. While Jesus was on his way to the house of a Centurion to heal one of the servants, he was met by some messengers sent by that Roman officer.

"Do not trouble further, sir; it is not for me to have you under my roof, and that is why I did not presume to approach you in person. But say the word and my servant will be cured "(Luke 7: 6-8 NEB).

As you probably know, when the messengers returned to the home of the centurion, they found the servant in good health. In this case Jesus was very impressed with the action of the Roman officer. He said to the crowd of people following him, "I tell you, nowhere, even in Israel, have I found faith like this." That Jesus came for all people was made evident in this story. The centurion was a gentile, a member of the hated Roman army and yet Jesus not only was willing to heal his servant, he also praised the man in public for his exemplary demonstration of faith.

51

One of the more difficult areas to understand in healing is Jesus' involvement with evil spirits. The dark side was real to Jesus. When he healed the sick, he often addressed the spirits whom he believed were causing the distress. Of course, that was the prevailing belief of that time, that disease was caused by evil spirits. We can explain some of these cases such as epilepsy as illnesses with a known physical cause, which we can control now with medication. However, we cannot ignore the fact that Jesus believed that he was dealing with spirit personalities, who appeared to recognize him and pleaded with him for mercy. The Bible records that Jesus drove out demons and instructed his followers to do the same. In the Gospel of Mark we read, "he summoned the Twelve and sent them out on a mission. He gave them authority over unclean spirits" (Mark 6: 7-8 NEB) and later on in that chapter it says that "They drove out many devils, and many sick people they anointed with oil and cured" (Mark 5: 13 NEB). Within the context of their times that was their explanation for the healing... if one was healed that meant that the unclean spirits had been cast out. Today we might say that when the negative attitudes of resentment, hate, guilt and fear had gone, people were healed. These can truly be thought of as unclean spirits which need to be removed so that healing can take place. There were no limits to what Jesus could do in the area of healing - and according to his promise to us, there should be no limits to what we should expect when we offer healing in his name. Some of the healings that Jesus did seem to go far beyond what we feel we can do. However, when people in healing circles get together and share their collective experiences, we hear of how the lame have walked, the blind have received their sight, withered and deformed hands have been restored and the sick have recovered from so-called "incurable" conditions such as cancer, arthritis, multiple sclerosis and heart disease, healings of mental illnesses and even the expulsion of evil spirits, real or imagined... in our time, as we have prayed in his name.

Chapter 5

Healing the Dark Side

In our time, evil spirits are usually considered something our ancestors created to explain phenomena that they could not understand. The spirit world was very prominent among primitive people. Everything was explained in terms of good and evil spirits. Spirits were in everything and could cause great harm to people. As such they needed to be appeased through offerings and sacrifices.

Today, we can explain natural phenomena such as electrical storms, earthquakes and volcanoes and know that they are not evil spirits expressing their displeasure with us. No longer do we build idols out of stone and clay to house some spirit of darkness. At the same time, we see people behaving in ways that are harmful to themselves and to others. A kind and loving man becomes transformed into an entirely different sort of person when he is enraged. Yes, we know that in each of us resides the capacity to choose good or evil. As we seek to follow Christ and receive the guidance of the Holy Spirit, we remain true to our higher selves and come across as decent people. But that is not really what we are talking about when we are dealing with evil spirits. We are talking about people being under attack by spiritual beings in the service of Evil, in our time. I used to regard that sort of thing as a fantasy in someone's mind. I have always believed in good counseling at the hands of reliable persons when someone has a problem and I still do.

However, there are some cases that confound the medical people and psychologists as well. The case of Hitler and his inner group of followers is hard to explain without taking evil into consideration. Could normal people perpetrate such crimes against humanity such as the extermination of millions of men, women and children without espousing the evil one? One might counter with an opinion that Hitler is a classic example of child abuse, having been beaten daily during his childhood. As in the case of other abused persons, he spent the rest of his life projecting that object of his abuse on others. Other factors such as the peculiarity of the German people to follow orders had been clearly planted in them as a normal condition of family life. The father (sometimes the mother) is in charge. Obedience is expected. So there is a possible explanation for that nation's people to blindly follow their leader even when doing so was against their own standards of right and wrong.

Today, we see evidence of interest in the Satanic in the current fascination with the occult. At the present time there has been the development of devil worship. One day my son and I were browsing through a bookstore, a very reputable place, when Phil pointed out to me a section on the occult, including a satanic bible. The use of drugs is widespread and crime abounds because of it. The arms race still seems to be out of control and such things as Watergate and the Iran-Contra deal occur in "the land of the free and the home of the brave". In the face of all these things we wonder if there is such a thing as satanic influence in our world. If we can entertain the possibility of evil spirits at work in our time, we should also recognize that we have authority over them. That is true even if the Devil and evil spirits exist only in our minds, for we are subject to what we believe. Though we may be unable to prove the existence of evil spirits, they are real to those who believe in them. Likewise, the remedy for casting them out is the same, whether they are imaginary or not.

The book and resulting film, *The Exorcist* [1] brought the possession of a person by an evil spirit to the attention of many people. Unfortunately, that was an extreme case, for actual possession of someone is very rare. Much more often we run into the situation where a person is harassed or oppressed by what they believe to be evil spiritual beings. Also, the movie seemed too much like just another horror movie to win many converts to a belief in that sort of thing.

However, in the course of my healing ministry I have occasionally dealt with persons who felt that they were being harassed or invaded by an unwelcome spirit. I have been asked by some to drive out the alien spirit as Jesus did. Without any special training in that type of spiritual therapy I used the method described in the New Testament. I spoke to the entity as though it were there and ordered it to leave. I said, "In the name of Jesus Christ leave this person and do not return again". Whenever I have done this I have noticed some reactions in the sick persons. Sometimes it appeared that they had assumed the personality of some dark spirit. In some cases the afflicted person took on a hostile appearance, expressed anger and ordered me to leave. Never-the-less, as long as I remained firm - sometimes repeating the order for them to leave, the sick persons were relieved and felt that they had been released from some kind of bondage.

I have also been asked to offer what is called

Deliverance Prayer for some persons at the request of their families or friends, who believed that their loved one was being oppressed in some way by a Satanic force. In those cases I did not attempt to address some entity directly but prayed for the Christ spirit to enter the sick one and give healing and protection. Authors, Matthew and Dennis Linn wrote the book, Deliverance Prayer in which they gave guidelines for persons seeking to pray in this manner for those who may be afflicted. Following is an excerpt from their book.

WHO MINISTERS DELIVERANCE ?
1. Everyone may pray self-deliverance prayer just as we do in praying the Our Father focusing on the Father's love and not on the fear of evil spirits. Christians can always exercise their baptismal power by silent prayer for others. Ideally the person receiving prayer should not be told that he has an evil spirit but simply that he is receiving silent prayer for the Lord's healing and blessing. Generally, silent deliverance prayer is sufficient.[2]

Historically, Christians have believed that they have all been given authority by Jesus Christ, to cast out evil spirits. On the basis of my office as an Episcopal priest I felt that I was following in the tradition of Jesus and his Disciples in using Deliverance Prayer on those who seemed to be under some oppression. Again, whether an evil spirit was actually present I cannot say. By their thoughts and actions they became subject to the idea of an evil invader. They turned over their power to an object of fear. Power was given back to them when they received Deliverance Prayer - when I acted with authority in Jesus' name.

Many believe that evil spirits do exist in our world

and cause grief to us human beings. Others feel that when individuals experience these things it is the product of their own minds. As in psychosomatic illnesses, where a person experiences all the trauma and pain of a real disease, those who believe they are under attack by an alien entity, feel all the anguish as acutely as if they were truly under another spirit's control. Dr Kenneth McAll, a former missionary-surgeon and presently a psychiatrist practicing in England, believes that some people do suffer from the presence of spirits, not necessarily evil spirits, but the spirits of those who have died and have not been able to make the transition to another life. There are many theories on why this is so, but McAll feels that the spirit's death may not have been properly dealt with in a spiritual manner, perhaps lacking a proper burial, as in the case of abortions or premature births - where these souls were not recognized as persons to be offered to God in prayer. In his book, Healing the Family Tree, [3] he gives some convincing evidence of persons being healed mentally and physically through taking care of, these disincarnate spirits, which he believes are still earthbound and are clinging to someone living here. Some remarkable healings occurred when McAll followed such simple practices as having one of the clergy offer a Eucharist for the dead for the earthbound spirit in question.

It is Dr. McAll's belief that some of these spirit entities have affected persons through three or four generations of a family tree. When he has suspected some influence from an earthbound spirit on one of his patients he has searched for evidence of problems back in that family tree. That has sometimes involved going back several generations to find a situation which is suspect - someone who died violently or was lost at sea without burial. Once discovered, he has asked for help from some pastor who could offer prayers of forgiveness and give a blessing in behalf of the earthbound spirit. In an attitude of love and forgiveness the deceased is committed to God, most often within the context of the Eucharist (Holy Communion)

Dr. Edith Fiore, a psychologist, has had many experiences similar to those of Dr McAll. Using hypnosis and directly dealing with these entities she has achieved success as she has assured them that they will be forgiven and accepted into God's loving arms - and sends them on with a blessing. She gives a good account of her experiences in her book, *THE UNQUIET DEAD : A PSYCHOLOGIST TREATS SPIRIT POSSESSION.*[4] Some years ago I had the opportunity to visit with the late Olga Worrall, the well known clairvoyant and healer, who with her husband, Ambrose, carried on a significant healing ministry in a Methodist Church in Baltimore, Maryland. She told me that she had personally encountered persons who had died, who were unaware of what had happened - momentarily drifting between the two states of existence. She gave them assurance of God's love and called to "helpers" who had made the transition to come and lead these disincarnate souls on to new life and experience in another realm.

When I learned of the positive results those persons had received, I began to use some of these practices in my own ministry. In cases where there had been a miscarriage or abortion I recommended to the mother in question that she give a name to the child and let us offer him/her into God's keeping. In addition to that I would offer a Eucharist in the name of the unborn fetus. In each case it had a calming and healing result in the woman who had been involved.

In another case friends of mine in Hawaii had seen a ball of fire about the size of a grapefruit, floating in the air and darting around the outside of their recently acquired home. Not really understanding this phenomenon they mentioned it to some of the island people who said it could be a departed spirit. They said it was a locally accepted belief that unhappy spirits occasionally appeared as balls of fire. On further investigation my friends learned that a person, suffering from alcoholism, experienced a painful death in that house, suffering from cancer of the liver. We decided to bless the house and its environs, concluding the blessing with a home Eucharist in which we offered prayers for the troubled spirit. There were no further sightings of the mysterious red ball and my friends felt happy and relaxed about their new place.

Following the example of Jesus, we can use a blessing to counter a curse, forgiveness in place of judgment and offer these gifts not only to the living but even to those who have already left their earthly bodies and are needing to make their transition to a higher realm. The healing touch is needed here in an area which continues to confound us even in this age of science and technology. We may not be able to believe in evil spirits as coming from the Prince of Darkness, but we should be able to understand how such mental and emotional states as FEAR, GUILT, HATE can take on the role of demons in persons' lives. Your compassion and love can drive out the fear. Being assured of God's forgiveness can remove the guilt and pave the way to the love that dispels the hate. Even in dealing with afflictions of the dark side your touch can heal.

Chapter 6

Limitations of Touch

After reading about the Jesus touch and the good reports we have received of those in both medical and spiritual healing, it appears that we should have no problem wiping out disease. However, whenever we are dealing with human beings we cannot take anything for granted. Today there are great advances in medicine with new techniques being developed every day. Organ transplants, once only a rare possibility, with slim hopes for success, are now routine with excellent success rates. People are exploring their own natural healing gifts and healing has made a comeback in the Church in this generation. In spite of all the positive developments, people are still suffering and dying from the diseases which continue to plague mankind. We get to a point when we think that through immunization we have just about eliminated the major life-threatening diseases such as polio, diphtheria, and small pox and AIDS comes out of nowhere to confound the medical experts.

One of our problems in combating illness is the fact that sickness has its rewards. Going back to our earliest memories, most of us remember being sick as a time when we received a lot of love and attention. In my own memory, some of the special times I remember with my mother during my childhood were the times when I was sick in bed. Instead of giving me toast as usual, my mom would cut it in strips and serve it as "a log cabin". She would sit by my bedside and read to me and in our family of five boys, that was a treat to receive such special attention. I really did have a fever and a sort throat, but I didn't care about that as long as I could receive all these other rewards.

I often visit the children's wards in our local hospitals. The kids there have every conceivable kind of game and toy to help them occupy their time while they are getting treatment away from home. Of course, when they first arrive they are apprehensive and following surgery they are sore, but in the recuperative stages, these children seem to be having lots of fun.

That special treatment does not stop as we become adults. You enter some these children seem to be having lots of sick rooms and are almost bowled over with the aroma of flowers. The patient greets you with a smile and offers you a chocolate from a box she has just received. Even if you live alone, a day of sick leave can be a time for you to "baby yourself', lying in bed with a pitcher of juice by your side, watching TV or reading a good book. As a result, we have developed a generation of people who want to be sick...not too sick, but still sick enough to have to stay in bed.

Another thing we do. We get sick to help us to get out of something we wish to avoid. Does that sound so preposterous to you? Hundreds of us do that every day. It begins when you are a child in school with that class you hate to attend - that exam you are not prepared for...and what do you know? "Mom, I have a stomach ache." Then as you grow older, that same mechanism is used to get you out of other difficulties, so you "call in sick". It may be that you can't stand one more day working under that new supervisor, or maybe you dread some project that is coming up at work. You are angry with your husband - so if he decides to be amorous, you might decide to come down with a headache. No, you really wouldn't consciously decide that at all...the headache would just come, and it would be real

Are these things premeditated consciously ? Of course not. "Me get sick on purpose ! Why that's ridiculous - I'm a responsible person...I wouldn't fake being ill." Also, it can become one of the methods people use to control others. Even serious illness can be used by a person to maintain control over the lives of the sick person's family. Dr. Bernie Siegel, a practicing surgeon and professor at Yale, sites an extreme case of this in his book, *Love, Medicine & Miracles.*

"Since physical illness usually brings sympathy from friends and relatives, it can be a way of gaining love, or nurturing. It can become a patient's only way of relating to the world, the only control one has over life. Gladys, a patient of mine who'd had a chronic intestinal inflammation for some fifty years, learned to manipulate her whole family this way. I met her after she developed cancer. The family looked sicker than she did, because she had some family member awake to wait on her twenty-four hours a day. Even when they hired a nurse to care for her, Gladys would awaken the family and let the nurse sleep. Over and over she developed severe pains at home, which mysteriously disappeared each time she was admitted to the hospital. (1)

In this story, Siegel later went on to say that his patient never wanted to be healed. There are many people like Gladys, who apparently need to be sick because the illness meets some needs which are important to them. There are others who need to continue in their illness for the same reason. That may have been true of the man at the pool of Bethesda. Jesus wondered about that himself.

Now at the Sheep-Pool in Jerusalem there is a place with five colonnades. Its name in the language of the Jews is Bethesda. In these colonnades there lay a crowd of sick people, blind, lame and paralyzed. Among them was a man who had been crippled for thirty-eight years. When Jesus saw him lying there and was aware that he had been ill a long time, he asked him, 'Do you want to recover?" 'Sir,' he replied, 'I have no one to put me in the pool when the water is disturbed, but while I am moving, someone else is in the pool before me.' Jesus answered, 'Rise to your feet, take up your bed and walk.' The man recovered instantly, took up his stretcher, and began to walk (John 5: 2-9 NEB).

When Jesus asked the man, "Do you want to recover," he knew that a healing would change the whole pattern of that man's life. After thirty-eight years of sitting by the pool, what would he do with himself? He might even develop an identity crisis. He would no longer be the helpless cripple living off of charity - but someone who should be gainfully employed... but doing what ? Healing would create new problems for him, requiring many adjustments in his life. That is also true of many who are sick today. A healing of their condition might well "rock the boat" in their lives. For years, Johnny has been excused from the chores the other children have been doing. Now, healed of his asthma, he must begin to take his turn.

I once saw a woman go from obscurity to become a celebrity of sorts - all because she became sick with cancer. A spinster, with one leg shorter than the other from polio, she had lived unnoticed and alone for years. Shy, she avoided the crowds and appeared only at the early service for church each week. Few knew her, that is, until she became sick. At that time, she became known to a group of persons interested in the healing ministry. One person made it her assignment to be the companion in the sick room, to fulfill all the duties done by the hospital "gray ladies" and also, just to be there. The clergy came to her regularly with communion and lay persons visited with frequency, ministering to her with the "laying on of hands" and treating her as a dear member of their own family. Would she trade good health for all of this attention? Never! Due to the caring services of that devoted group of Christians, Evelyn reigned like a queen over her sick room. The more her body weakened, the more her mind and spirit flourished. Even her funeral was a grand occasion for that Canadian lass as a Scottish bagpiper led the procession into the church. I suppose that if Jesus had asked Evelyn, "Do you want to recover?" she might have replied, " No thank you, Lord, I'm really enjoying the healing of my mind and spirit. Since my illness I have been nurtured with more love than I have known in my entire life."

We shall say more about cases like Evelyn's when we get to Chapter 8, "Touch for the Dying". We know that there is a time to die and we have learned, as in the story above, that there are many good things we can do for those who are facing death. However, there are still too many people out there who are sick, who shouldn't be sick at all. They insist upon being ill even with the best of doctors, good medications and available spiritual and mental resources. What are the impediments to healing? Under similar conditions and using the same medical and/or spiritual therapy, why does one patient get well and another person show little or no improvement - may even die?

Dr. 0. Carl Simonton, a medical doctor and Stephanie Matthews, a psychologist, made a great deal of progress with so-called *terminal* cancer patients by using imaging techniques. Their methods are described in a book they wrote with James L. Creighton titled *Getting Well Again*[2]. Their results were amazing. In a group of 159 patients, who were "supposed to die", 19 percent actually recovered with another 22 percent in different stages of regression. Even those who died had shown signs of improvement and lengthened their predicted time remaining. Imaging involves using our minds by visualizing places which would be ideal for our enjoyment and health. Also a patient might use his imagination to see his own white blood cells fighting and defeating the cancer cells in his body. In prayer therapy, we visualize a tumor shrinking as we offer our healing touch.

Following the Simonton approach, Bernie Siegel, M.D., mentioned above, began a therapy group called Exceptional Cancer Patients (ECaP) to expand the base of support for people fighting that disease. In his medical practice, he had seen individuals overcome cancer where it had seemed impossible. He noted certain characteristics about these survivors that were different from the others - they were exceptional. Rather than to be drowning in a sea of despair they were angry, angry with the disease and not about to accept the doctor's prognosis. He found out that these exceptional patients had a great desire to live a long time. They had faith in something or someone and they were determined to make it. Encouraged by what he had seen, he organized the ECaP group, using *Getting Well Again* as a resource book. Now Siegel and his own books are getting attention for the ECaP group has enjoyed great success.

Through the medium of video tapes, cancer patients everywhere have been able to join with Bernie and his ECaP friends. His tape, "Fight for Your Life" is a step by step program, which teaches people how to become survivors and is designed to be used daily over and over again. * Support for his ideas and program are coming from many directions. The session I attended was held on the island of Kauai and among those in attendance were doctors, nurses, psychologists, ministers and lay persons, some with serious illnesses. Joining with him at this workshop were Dr. Gerald Jampolsky, author of *Love is Letting go of Fear*,[3], Dr. Donald Pachuta, and Dianne Cirincione.

That is what is happening in some parts of the medical world, the attempt to get people to use their own inner resources, with help coming from others who are also fighting for their lives. The success of such programs has been clearly demonstrated by Alcoholics Anonymous. Their famous Twelve-Step program has exploded into a network of groups dealing with other kinds of addictions. There are others there to help, like Simonton, Siegel and Jampolsky. If more clergy were to involve themselves in these programs, they would be a welcome addition, offering hope to those facing life or death. From the religious side, we who have been given the divine commission to heal, know that "our help comes from the Lord". That is a message that needs to be shared with those attempting to become survivors. They are learning to fight for themselves. They are learning to have faith in their support groups. They need to learn, that in addition to these, they are upheld by the same power that upholds the universe. That is what we all need to hear, whether we are in crisis or not.

In an effort to learn about the power of prayer, Dr. William Parker, a psychologist, made a study of prayer in the fifties with his students at Redlands University. In 1957, Parker and Elaine St..Johns reported their findings in a book called, *Prayer Can Change Your Life* [4]. I was encouraged when I recently read that book, for it affirmed many of my own findings which I have been sharing with you. At the outset the authors say, as I said earlier, that the first requirement for healing is to enter the kingdom within. That is true for the healer as well as the one in need of healing.

Parker's studies revealed that within a person's unconscious mind there could be hidden fears, inferiority feelings, feelings of guilt and feelings of hostility that could trigger other kinds of illnesses. Simonton and Matthews had noticed the presence of some of these negative attitudes in their cancer patients. Above I said that there are times when we become sick conveniently to avoid some unpleasant situation. We are quite unaware of our part in producing that illness. Likewise, we are unaware of the unresolved guilt and hostilities which have gathered within our unconscious.

We need to be honest when we enter within, for our purpose is to discover those inhibiters to health we have been hiding from ourselves for years. Knowing that it can truly be a matter of our own life or death gives us the courage to do it. You can go on for years unable to quit smoking, but if the doctor says to you, "You either quit smoking or it will kill you," you will most likely drop it overnight.

We need to educate the general public concerning these concepts in the same way they have been taught the importance of good sanitation, clean air and good diet for health. In fact, I believe that the poisons lurking within our unconscious are more life-threatening than the more obvious physical pollutants. When it comes to spiritual healing such as prayer therapy with the laying on of hands and/or anointing, we know that certain attitudes are necessary to provide a climate for healing. In essence these necessary elements serve as antidotes to those inhibiters above; FEAR, GUILT, HATE and INFERIORITY FEELINGS.

Where do we find these hidden feelings? How do we unearth forgotten memories which may be eroding the inner structures of our minds? Up until now we have been afraid to look inside ourselves directly. That is one of the purposes of dreams. Through symbols and stories they reveal what is important for us to know about ourselves. Yet, most people put aside their dreams casually as the result of "something I ate last night". Whenever we are in the midst of a personal crisis, when an important decision is needed, we may get some help from examining our dreams. The following example may serve to clarify.

Some years ago I was given a chance to run for a national position for an organization in which I believed. The position would be in addition to my regular job, which was in Alaska. I would have to make frequent trips around the country, trips which would involve speeches and conferences requiring preparation. It all sounded very tempting to me, but at the same time I wondered if I could handle the elective position and my job as well. While I was in the midst of that quandary I had the following dream.

Rosalyn Jackson, the gentle and appealing wife of a young accountant, came to me obviously upset. She said, "Malcolm, I'm really worried about Steve. He seems determined to go ahead with his plans and if he does, Father Elliott says he will have to shoot him. Father says, 'It's nothing personal...it's the law! If Steve breaks the law, I'll have to shoot him.' Please, Malcolm, help me convince Steve that he shouldn't do it."

I had been praying for guidance in my decision and the dream appeared. It seemed ridiculous at first with Father Elliott shooting someone, something completely out of character for the kindly priest. I went over the dream with my daughter, Donna, to see if we could make sense out of it. First, she said, " I think Rosalyn represents your *anima* the sensitive female side of yourself and Steve, her husband, what do you think of him?" "Let's see, now - I see Steve as a very ambitious young man, a driver, destined to go places." "Yes," she replied, "and probably in this case he stands for your Ego, the side of your personality that seeks acclaim." I answered, " I can see that, but how does Father Elliott fit into this? I really can't see him in the role of some kind of executioner." Donna then asked me, "Dad, what does Father Elliott stand for to you? What role does he play among the clergy of our diocese?" I went over it in my mind: Norman Elliott was one of our senior priests, a traditionalist who stood firmly by the faith, one who had served as parliamentarian at our church conventions... the interpreter of the law ! "Aha, I've got the answer now," I exclaimed. Very simply and clearly, my dream was telling me that if I went ahead with my plans, I should

71

have to pay for it. It would be a case of burning the candle at both ends. My *anima* was making herself known to me as the intercessor and naturally, I was ready to listen to such an engaging young lady. Just as every male has an *anima,* likewise every female has a male side within her who is referred to as the *animas* As we continue in our quest for wholeness, it is important to get in touch with the male or female counterparts within. Father Elliott's personality, serving as a symbol, was there to remind me that when we defy the law, even the laws pertaining to good judgment, we should be prepared to suffer the consequences. Incidentally, I did not need to concern myself about the national office I was seeking. I was not elected!

Jack Sanford's , *Dreams, God's Forgotten Language* [5] can be helpful in learning how to understand and use your dreams to good effect. Also, meditation and prayer are other means of helping us to get in touch with our inner mind and to receive direction from on high. I'm talking about the silent, listening prayer, not the kind where you are doing all the talking - not giving God a chance to say a thing.

Of the four inhibiters to healing, FEAR, GUILT, HATE AND INFERIORITY FEELINGS, perhaps, fear is the most common negative factor to control our thinking and actions (I am speaking of unreasoned fear, not the fear we feel when running from a bear or the awesome feeling we might have in the presence of God). Once a fear is recognized, it does not strike as much terror in your heart. To place a fear or some dreaded past memory on the table where it can be scrutinized, takes away much of its power. Love is the antidote to fear. Love from your pastor, your doctor, your support group, can give you the courage to *enter within*. Love is the most important element in the healing process. That is why Bernie Siegel is attempting to influence physicians to become more human with their patients, to give a hug, to care. That is the power we feel the most in prayer groups who gather around a sick person. Jesus taught that love could take away fear and demonstrated that in his caring manner with people.

GUILT is another factor that may be responsible for illness in some part of our body. Again, it is the guilt that is hidden from us that is the problem. When an experience is fresh in our minds we are in a position to deal with it. If it is a matter of calling someone and telling her that you are sorry, it can be dispensed with easily. You say, "I'm sorry," and she forgives and the guilt goes away as well. However, those unresolved hurts, some going all the way back to your childhood - they are the ones which can create an ulcer, a backache or a migraine headache or possibly something more serious.

A psychiatrist will get you to talk and may use hypnosis to help you to find your problems within. That could involve a look at your dreams and the therapy would probably last a long time. In spiritual healing we have a kind of inner healing named by the late Agnes Sanford, the healing of memories. To seek out the unhappy memory we utilize our imagination and ask the patient to go back through the years to that difficult time. Often, such memories are those involving some kind of child molestation or incest. Until recently, it was not considered good taste to bring up such matters. As a result, the experience lay there in the unconscious festering like a sliver under the skin. If the thought did come to mind, typically, the one who was attacked has carried the guilt, even though she was the injured party.

Christian therapists always bring Jesus into inner healing. Once the sick person has vividly recalled the unhappy memory, we ask them to *see* Jesus in the picture as well. We let them know that he is there to heal, even though the incident may have occurred years previously. Over and over, we find persons healed in this way. It usually involves forgiveness on the part of the one seeking healing, forgiveness for the offender, which is not easy to do. The case for inner healing. rests on the belief that God can transform that which is harmful into something useful. For example, if a person who was molested, learns from that bad experience and becomes a counselor to others, the sin has been transformed into a positive purpose. Most of the volunteer counselors working with the victims of rape are persons who themselves have been raped. Likewise, AA guides and counselors to those overcoming alcoholism were victims of that disease themselves. The greatest example of God's transforming the worst to the best is the story of Jesus' crucifixion and resurrection. From Friday, the darkest day in the history of mankind, we move to Easter Sunday, the day of victory and promise for all of us.

HATE joins FEAR and GUILT as a cause of sickness and a barrier to healing. Usually we work on the elimination of hate as we remove guilt. God's promise of forgiveness brings about a healing at the same time we are released from guilt. The sick person may have stubbornly resisted forgiving his/her offenders and must be told that the continued hate no longer can make an impact on the offender. Instead, the unresolved hatred turns back on him and becomes his "growing ulcer". A spiritual guide is often necessary to help persons overcome a hostility that has been festering for years.

INFERIORITY FEELINGS are present in all of us to some degree. Sometimes, in an effort to keep us modest, our parents and friends have been too critical of us, making us feel insecure. "Don't let it go to your head ! You braggart, you! You think you're smart...well you aren't smart, you're stupid, yes, stupid !" How many times have you heard things like that ? Probably you heard things like that from your older brothers and sisters - also your peers. Children can be vicious the way they taunt one another.

Such feelings of inferiority can slow us down on life's journey. They can make us veer away from our true potential. We may start out in pursuit of our dream, only to have our hopes dashed along the way by the caustic barbs of others. A low self-image can stop us in our tracks. We can feel so unworthy that we think we do not deserve healing. We deserve to die, so we do not respond to medications or to healing prayer. Some are so convinced of their worthlessness that they take their own lives. Others make their suicide respectable and die from cancer or starve themselves. We must learn again that each one of us was made in the image of God for a purpose. Somehow, it is important to God and the universe that we become what we were born to be.

I had many of these ideas in mind when I created The Rejoice Plan, an affirmation card contained within my book, *Healing and the Abundant Life.*[3] The affirmation card begins by emphasizing the uniqueness of each of us as God's creation, here to live a life with a plan. We must love. We must forgive and last but not least, we not forget how to dream great dreams.

75

Earlier in this chapter we mentioned how expectancy and hope were essential for Bernie's ECaP patients. The rewards are there to be accepted. With faith, with intelligent thinking, with the expulsion of all the garbage from our minds, with forgiving hearts, with good medical and spiritual guides, and with the love of our friends and support groups we can expect our reward that of healing and wholeness, in one way or another.

Chapter 7

The Hurtful Touch

We have heard of the blessings of touch, how gentle hands nurture others, giving comfort and relaxation...even healing. Charlie Brown might say that "Happiness is being hugged and squeezed". That is touch at its best. However, we all know too well that there is another side of touch which is evil - the touch that hurts. Those very hands which can offer warmth and healing can be used as weapons which inflict pain on others.

I remember how shocked I was to see a badly bruised face and body and realize that she was one of my friends, a member of our church. She had been severely battered by her husband. Besides being in pain, she had trouble focusing her eyes. She was experiencing double vision and her doctor thought I might be able to help. I remember that I used a form of therapeutic touch with prayer, allowing my hands to be guided around her head and before her eyes. She came out of her state of relaxation being able to see clearly only one Malcolm Miner standing by her bedside.

After years of denial, the ugly facts of child abuse and battered wives, husbands too, are now known to be all too common in our society. Rape is another crime in which one or more persons are brutal to another. Who are these persons who are doing these vicious things? Certainly, they must be evil through and through - to maim their babies and beat their wives half to death. The sad fact is that they are like you and me. Often they are decent folk, who are respected among their friends and associates. Some are practicing Christians, who feel pain and remorse for their actions, once they have come to their senses. Certain cases involve the use of drugs or alcohol. A significant number of abusers are persons who were abused themselves, those who never received enough love in their formative years.

When we hear of these terrible deeds, we become angry and wish to punish those responsible. Unfortunately, that is not an answer that will take care of the problem. We can punish certain types of abusers, such as serial killers, through the courts. However, even these extreme types are usually persons who have been rejected over and over again to a point where whatever capacity there is for love, turns to hate. Most abusers are normal people most of the time, but under tension they lose control and inflict pain on those they love. The answer to their problem comes with understanding and love and forgiveness... and that is hard for us to do. Not only do they need our forgiveness but they must learn to love themselves. They need to have good feelings about themselves before they can treat others in a wholesome manner.

Secular organizations were the first to take positive action on such matters as child abuse and wife battering. Shelters were established to provide counseling and comfort for the afflicted, and these have also provided counseling for the abusers themselves. Of course, churches have been involved through their human service programs, but caring people in the secular world were first on the scene. As a minister, I feel that the Church should always be first to respond to a human need, but sadly, that is not the case.

The Church I know is not always the most loving body in dealing with others and their failings. While we are enjoying the love and acceptance of our friends in our home parish, we often have no problem judging others outside our intimate group. It is sad to say that even though we believe we are redeemed through the forgiveness and acceptance of Jesus, that sometimes we are unable to pass on that love and acceptance to everyone. We make distinctions as to whom we shall forgive, whom we shall punish...whom we shall allow into our group. Once safely in the fellowship of the Church, we are in danger of falling into the trap of judging others. It is the same temptation which entrapped some of the Pharisees in the time of Jesus' ministry. To them, the law was the law and those who broke it were to be punished, period. Jesus was seen as an upstart and a threat when he suggested the way of love and forgiveness as an alternative to the punishment prescribed by the law.

Jesus stopped the execution of an adulteress by reminding those who were about to stone her of their own frailties (John: 8: 1-11). Though the prevailing law meant that she should be punished, he defied those who were eager to stone her to death. When he said to them, "the one of you who is without sin throw the first stone," he disarmed them. There was not a one of them who could handle judgment if it was his own sin that was in question. Needless to say, they hung their heads and went away in silence.

Jesus brought to the world a message of love and forgiveness and healing. He really loved people and felt for them in their needs and suffering. He was the most understanding teacher the world has ever known, full of compassion for those who were hurting and offering forgiveness for those who had gone astray. Possessing all authority to judge, he was the most non-judgmental of all teachers when it came to the normal "sins of the flesh", such as sexual sins, gluttony and drunkenness. Yet, many of today's Christians would say that the worst of all sins have to do with drinking and sex. Jesus was more concerned about how people treated one another. Sins were those errors which separated us from each other and from God. When Jesus spoke as a judge, his statements were reserved for such as the Pharisees, where he attacked their hypocrisy and unbending attitudes.

He was criticized for associating with publicans and sinners and for socializing with them in the pubs of that day. He was attacked for allowing a woman of questionable reputation to publicly wash his feet and anoint them. When the little man called Zacchaeus could not see Jesus until he climbed a tree, our Lord honored him by choosing his home for his visit. The down trodden, the humble and lowly, the sick and those of ill repute; those were the ones who received special attention from Jesus Christ.

When it is in the context of the Bible, it is not difficult for us to relate to Jesus. However, if we were to bring him into our contemporary world, we might have a hard time adjusting to him. Think of Jesus, in the midst of a group of "street people". He would be right at home, but would we ? Can you imagine him being friends with drunks and prostitutes and treating them on a par with us *solid citizens* and church members? That would be hard for many of us to take, and many would deny him as Lord, just because of his questionable associations.

Likewise, it was difficult for the religious leaders of his time to understand Jesus. The Prophets and Holy Men such as John the Baptist were persons who denied their physical natures so that they could grow spiritually. Though Jesus had times when he fasted, he did so for a special purpose, as in the beginning of his ministry. However, in his normal life Jesus was not an ascetic. Neither did he teach asceticism. We have no examples where he urged others to deny their instinctive, bodily natures.

He came to offer the abundant life to everyone, but not all were prepared to accept his gift. The leaders of the established religion of that time were ready to criticize Jesus at every turn. They rejected him and his gifts. He was even downgraded for his healing when he did it on the Sabbath. They were the kinds of people who lived by every *jot and tittles* of the Law, and knew nothing of the spirit of the law. They were the most judgmental of persons, those who would demand "an eye for an eye and a tooth for a tooth" whenever someone had made a mistake.

There are people like that in the world today. It is sad to say that a significant number of them are to be found in the religious establishments. I truly believe that judging is one of the serious sins of religious people - but then, it always has been so.

I was once asked to go to the hospital to visit a person, dying of cancer. The reason I was asked to go ? The patient had been abandoned by members of her congregation. They had prayed over her and had taken the position that she should claim the healing as a victory over sin and Satan. They believed that all she had to do was accept the healing, rise from the hospital bed and go home well. She did not have the faith ... it was her fault, as far as they were concerned. She had not met the conditions they expected of a practicing Christian. So they stopped visiting her and she would have had to face her last days alone, if another friend had not discovered her in her plight.

In spite of her dire predicament, judging still entered in, though the sick person was suffering and in obvious distress. She really needed someone to be there...to hold her hand and be Jesus for her. For that is what we are called to do, to try to give the love, the forgiveness, the comfort that Jesus would give if he were at that bedside. Of course, we know that he would also give healing, by a simple touch or simply by command. Being something less than perfect, we cannot always bring healing to the sick, but we can let them know that we care and that they are not alone. The last thing we need to be is judgmental.

Judgment comes into play whenever our personal sense of morality is offended. In the late eighties the American public was subjected to charges of immorality and fraud brought against television evangelist, Jim Bakker and his PTL (Praise the Lord) organization The PTL scandal was sad, not only because the critics were judgmental : they seemed to revel in it. No one who understands human nature should be surprised to learn that a Christian leader can be guilty of sin. One definition of sin is "missing the mark" - and do not we all fail to live up to our best intentions at times? Traditionally, Jesus has been accepted as one without sin (did not "miss the mark"). When we become

Christians we believe that our former sins are forgiven, but that does not mean we shall not sin again. Jesus loved the sinner and gave his life for him. Jesus loves Jim Bakker and forgave him a long time ago. What kind of people are we if we cannot do the same?

It is sad that the public can get so excited about another's fall from grace. The jokes that made us laugh were unkind and the press and the TV comedians may have overdone it at the expense of the evangelists caught up in that sad affair. Hopefully, by the time this is read, many will have remembered the good that Jim and Tammy Bakker did for lonely people and shut-ins who were cheered by the hopeful messages on their programs through the years. I hope that those who had rocks in their hands will have been reminded of what Jesus said about casting that first stone. Maybe some day we will want Jesus to come to our rescue. It will be comforting at that time to remember that we were among those who forgave and forgot.

Today we are living in a world where human behavior is out in the open. "The pill" offered not only protection from pregnancy, but opened Pandora's box of previously suppressed sexual information and practices in our society. New attitudes regarding sexual freedom and expression have created new problems for our generation. With it there emerged the Gay Revolution, bringing homosexuals out from under cover to demand their rights and place in the sun. A homosexual person may be considered as a sinner by someone, as one with an illness by another and one who has merely chosen an alternate life style by a third person.

In my opinion, we do not have all the answers on the subject of homosexuality. There seems to be strong evidence that it is genetic in origin. In our society members of churches differ strongly when it comes to the subject of gays. Churches are split over the gay issue on the subject of ordination of gay men and women and over the matter of blessing same sex partnerships. Basically, the Fundamentalist groups cite the Bible as the authority which condemns homosexuality as immoral. In the first chapter of the Apostle Paul's Letter to the Romans, he describes what he believes to be the depravity of the Gentiles. "Their women have exchanged natural intercourse for unnatural, and their men in turn, giving up natural relations with women, burn with lust for one another; males behave indecently with males, and are paid in their own persons the fitting wage of such perversion" (Romans 1:26-28,NEB). However, though the previous quotation by Paul really is an attack on homosexual behavior, it is only one sentence in a larger paragraph describing pagan idolatry, which included various kinds of sexual acts in its worship. In the pagan temples there were priest/prostitutes who had sex with men as acts of worship and there were females, priestess/prostitutes, who were having sex with women. Paul was specifically aiming his criticism at pagan prostitution in the temples. The reference to their being paid shows that these offenders were indeed temple prostitutes. Paul was revolted by everything these Canaanites were doing, carving graven images to worship and behaving badly in every way. "They are filled with every kind of injustice, mischief, rapacity and malice: they are one mass of envy, murder, rivalry, treachery and malevolence; whisperers and scandal mongers, hateful to God. (Romans 1:29-31, NEB). Paul sounds a little like the Ayatollah Khomeini did when he was describing

84

American Christians, as reported by the media on Television. That Islamic leader saw America as a nation dominated by Satanic rule, a people who used alcohol and other drugs, where women exposed their bodies shamelessly, where the youth danced to music which aroused the sexual emotions...on and on and on. To the Ayatollah we must have looked much like the Gentiles of old as viewed by the apostle, Paul, who saw homosexual practices only within the context of the depraved Canaanite culture and its use of prostitutes in its religious practices. In his time there was nothing in that society which approximated the present day practice of two adults of the same sex living together in a committed relationship. When someone uses the above passage from Romans to prove to me that homosexuality is wrong I like to quote another passage Paul wrote in his letter to the Galatians. As many of you as were baptized into Christ have clothed yourselves with Christ. There is no longer Jew or Greek, there is no longer slave or free, there is no longer male and female, for all of you are one in Christ Jesus"(Galatians: 3:28 RSV).

I was given a closer view of the Gay Community than many when a nephew of mine became ill and subsequently died of AIDS. I was privileged to share with him and his family as he dealt with his life and approaching death. I was able to observe him and others living the gay lifestyle and came to the conclusion that those whom I met were sensitive and caring of others. Leaving sex aside, I found them to be good persons, morally and spiritually. My nephew, Gary, shared with me his thoughts about God and the meaning of life. He was a handsome, artistic, talented, intelligent, spiritual and loving person. I was convinced that he was a good person, really a special kind of person, who loved his God and was loved in return. A Catholic priest and I shared this belief with his family and friends at his memorial service. There are many ways of looking at this subject and if I must take a stand, it must be on the side of love and mercy rather than on the side of judgment. Those involved in this lifestyle are in need of God's love and healing grace as much as anyone. I have known many sincere clergymen and devout lay persons who were homosexuals, who gave competent and meaningful service to the church and society. Personally I see the present homophobia concerning the gay community as a fear and a reaction to something different, something not understood, something frightening. And because gays are in the minority it is easy to control them, abuse them and put them down.

Of course, there are some persons with serious problems, who have sexual perversions such as child abusers, who may prey upon innocent children These are in a different category. Often perverts are heterosexuals who have been cut off from their normal outlets. There are many gradations of sexual behavior for both gays and straights. We hear wild stories of sexual misbehavior at clubhouses. We hear of pickup bars and "one night stands" for men and women. Certainly, we cannot see how this cheapening of a primary instinct and life force can be of any value. Good sex always should involve love and commitment. Those involved in a kind of loveless sexual behavior devalue themselves and others and cannot help having a poor self image and low esteem. Many of these persons are ill and in need of therapy and when appropriate, the healing sacrament of reconciliation.

Some Christian therapists, like Francis and Judith MacNutt believe that homosexuality is an illness which can be healed by counseling and prayer. I heard them address that subject at a conference in Halifax, Nova Scotia in 1988. Judith stated that when prayer was used that she had experienced 100 percent healing of homosexuals. She went on to say that often that condition was based on an unmet need for the love of the parent of the same sex and that God can supply the love which that person had not received from his/her parents.

Even so, many physicians and psychologists will protest that homosexuality is not an illness but a fact of one's being, who one is rather than what one does. A person who has chosen that lifestyle will ask, "Why should I ask for healing when I am not sick?" So the debate continues. Personally, I am not offended by those who choose to live the gay life. As I said previously, homosexuals that I have had personal dealings with have proven to be as reliable as so-called "straight" people I have known. I have come to know them as "people" human beings, who are subject to doing right and wrong, good or bad like anyone. As one who has opted to follow Jesus, I cannot conceive of him not accepting and loving gays in the same way he loved everyone. That is very important for them, because when they receive judgment and in some cases, abuse, from some religious groups, they need to feel the love and acceptance of those members of Church and society who are on their side.

The typical reaction of the Church to most of these problems has been one of judgment rather than mercy. Some of these issues are far more complex than people wish to make of them. We who are in healing must begin to see people not for what they seem to be, but as human beings in need of love and understanding. There are plenty of people to do the judging...more than enough. Jesus is calling for some of us to follow his direction as a people who care.

After twenty years of marriage I found myself involved in a divorce. Even under the best of circumstances, where the individuals involved are trying to act charitably towards one another, there is hurt - there are misunderstandings - there is judgment. I found out that my actions had hurt others apart from my immediate family. Some of my friends in the Church felt that I had let them down. In their eyes I had not measured up - I had "missed the mark". Though I was fully aware that their approval of me had been brought about by my own actions, and sometimes I felt that I deserved it, I still felt the pain in their rejection. I am glad to say that the great majority of my friends in the church, including my ecclesiastical authorities, were understanding, caring, and forgiving. I experienced first hand the family of the Church as the fellowship of the redeemed.

To counsel and to heal takes people who can be objective and can listen to others without pronouncing judgment upon them. Jesus hated the sin, but never had anything but love and compassion for the sinner. There is not a single example where Jesus was harsh with those who were presumed to be guilty of the "sins of the flesh". The only time he appeared to be really angry was the time he drove the money lenders from the Temple - and these were people who were working under the direction of the Temple priests. He hated hypocrisy, he hated injustice, he hated sin and disease, because of the misery they brought to people. He loved children, he loved the common folk, he loved the others too...even his enemies. If he is our example, can we do less ? At least we can make a sincere effort to love one another.

Chapter 8

Therapeutic Touch

I moved my hands over the burn victim's body. He said, "What are you doing? I can feel something on my back wherever your hands move."

"Does it hurt? I'm not really touching you - you see, my hands are at least six inches from your back."

"No," he responded. "It feels good...like tingles all over me."

The next day, his doctors were impressed with the dramatic improvement in his condition. He was eventually released without requiring any skin grafts.

My granddaughter, Marsha, was burned at home and her mother used the same technique with her with the same outstanding results. Again in her case, the physician marveled at the improved condition of her skin.

What were we doing? It is a healing technique known as the therapeutic touch, a system developed and taught by Dolores Krieger, Ph.D., R.N., Professor of Nursing at New York University. Many of us have been familiar with the healing therapy known as the "laying on of hands", where the healer's hands are placed directly on a sick person. Often the hands are placed on the spot where the patient has a problem, as in the case of "tennis elbow", where the elbow is placed in the healer's hands while he/she prays. The therapeutic touch makes use of one's hands in healing, but in quite a different way. Professor Krieger has been traveling around the country, teaching nurses on the use of the *therapeutic touch* and eventually made her way to my home town , Anchorage, Alaska. I did not even know about her visit, but as I mentioned previously, my daughter, Linda heard of it through the School of Nursing at the University of Alaska and enrolled in the class.

Linda turned out to be an immediate success with the *therapeutic touch* method, being able to use it effectively from the beginning. In her excitement she soon shared this technique with her sister, Donna and with me. For us, it was merely a different way of using the laying on of hands, something we all had been involved in for some time.

Though the name, therapeutic touch suggests touching, with this method the healer's hands pass over the sick person, using a continuous motion and pausing over the area of infection or distress. The purpose is to deal with the energy field which immediately surrounds the human body. Advocates of this method believe that even the flow of energy over the surface of the skin can become congested and can be unruffled as the hands move over and around the body of the sick person. Those who use this method have all had common experiences which indicate that this type of touch relaxes the patient, often can relieve pain and generally assists the body in the healing process.

In an earlier chapter I described how Linda and Donna administered the therapeutic touch to my badly sprained ankle in such a way that the pain left me, the swelling went down and I was walking on it the very next morning. As soon as Linda had taken the course she began testing the method with her patients. In our home the laying on of hands was a common practice and she had used this whenever it had seemed appropriate in her nursing profession. When she tried the *therapeutic touch* as a variation of her prayer therapy, her results were as good or better than they were when she used the laying on of hands.

Dr. Krieger has explained her touch method in her book, *The Therapeutic Touch*. The book is easy to read and can be used as a "do it yourself" course, to some degree. That is particularly true if a person has had some experience in other areas of healing. On the back of the paper bound edition there is a good explanation of her method.

"Whether it be to relieve a headache, calm a muscle spasm, sooth a crying baby, or alleviate your own abdominal cramps, THE THERAPEUTIC TOUCH shows you how you can use your hands to help or to heal someone who is sick. Viewing therapeutic touch as a natural potential in all human beings, this book presents actual case studies and numerous self-tests to help you understand and perfect the technique of touching. Dr. Krieger shows you how to detect when a person is sick, pinpoint where the pain is, and stimulate the recuperative powers of the sick person. With accurate descriptions of the changes that take place in body temperature, levels of consciousness and physiology during this intense interaction, this book helps you interpret your healing experience and get the most meaning from it. In lieu of the many expensive, impersonal methods that help to make us well today, THE THERAPEUTIC TOUCH recaptures a simple, ancient mode of healing and shows how you can now become an integral part of your own or someone else's healing process."[1]

The *therapeutic touch* method has proven itself well enough for New York University to endorse it, offering it as a fully accredited graduate course at the master's level. As taught by Dolores Krieger, it is an additional resource for nurses to use with their patients. She does not consider it a religious practice and because of that, some Christian healers have been suspicious of her method. They are concerned that this might be some occult practice, as used by shamans and medicine men.

When we become involved with healing practices which rely on *going within* to our intuitive resources we are entering areas which have been used throughout the history of mankind. We find that some techniques in healing have been used universally by peoples of different religions and cultures. To Dr. Krieger her method is a non-sectarian approach, one that appeals to the best in human beings. In the case of *therapeutic touch* as offered by New York University, we are learning how to use certain natural gifts possessed by all of us. As in all gifts, some turn out to be more talented than others. And some become more proficient through study and experience. Dolores Krieger teaches her students to "center in". If someone asked me to "center in" before I ministered to a sick person, I'd assume an attitude of prayer. To Dolores it means to clear the mind of all the distractions of the surrounding environment and become receptive to your inner resources.

In secular practice, *therapeutic touch* is taking advantage of the natural healing abilities in human beings. When one uses that kind of *healing touch,* that which appears to occur is an interchange of some kind of energy from one person to another. The healer initially scans the body in search of an area where there is a change of temperature. When that area is found, the healer hovers over that place and may lay his/her hands on that spot. It is quite common for the patient to feel a sensation of heat during the time of concentrated effort. Likewise, many can register some kinds of feelings as the healer's hands are scanning their bodies. Other feelings experienced are feelings of peace, relaxation and sometimes a feeling of being loved, for the *therapeutic touch* is always given to the sick person in a caring way. In a very real sense, we are offering ourselves for the relief of those in need. Such loving actions as that are honored by the Lord of the Universe whether - they are offered in secular or religious terms. Regardless of the method, love is needed, as well as faith and hope.

"Krieger's Krazies", as she kiddingly refers to her associates, achieve the same good results in healing as the religious therapists, working with patients who have similar illnesses. God uses the natural gifts of physicians regularly and he can bless nurses when they use their natural talents with the *therapeutic touch.* Healing gifts are not unlike other gifts such as artistic or musical gifts. Our talents were given to us to be used and that includes healing talents.

As one who uses the therapeutic touch with prayer and the *laying on of hands* and sometimes anointing, I feel that I have some advantage over those who do it strictly relying on their own gifts. When we pray , expecting to receive "power from on high", it takes the pressure off of us. We do not need to be strong, for we are depending on the Holy Spirit to do the healing, using us as channels of his grace. I have used prayer therapy effectively with others even though I was ill myself. I think that when one is using a purely secular approach to healing, there is the danger of relying only on "the method of John", mentioned in Chapter 2, where the healer relies on his own strength of thought to accomplish the healing. I am aware that Dr. Krieger's method does emphasize going within, which is much closer to the "the method of Jesus", which relies on faith and prayer.

There are some doctors who resent the use of other resources than medical with their patients. They either ignore or discourage the involvement of clergy or lay persons who might be involved in a hospital ministry. On the other hand, there are Christians who feel that the only healing that is justified is healing in the name of Jesus Christ. It has been my experience that the best results come when we all work together for the good of the sick person.

In our present society the medical professions make up the majority of persons working with the sick. I could not name all of the many different kinds of physicians at work in the healing arts, doctors specializing in most anything you can name... the list goes on: nurses, pharmacists, physical therapists, bacteriologists, psychiatrists, those in research in pharmacology and immunology - and all the others in medical services. These people are all serving God as *ministers of healing,* even though they may be unaware of this.

My physician father had very little to say on that subject and considered his medical discipline one thing and his faith another. Yet, God helped my father use his natural talents to bring his patients to wholeness. My mother worked as a nurse for years without ever using the laying on of hands with prayer in a formal sense. Yet, as a dedicated Christian and believer she always prayed silently for her patients. She would have been happy to have known of the *therapeutic touch,* for with that knowledge, she could have added abundantly to the relief of her patients.

Let me share a story with you. I was asked to call on a young man in the hospital who was suffering with a great deal of pain. He did not seem to respond well to the sedatives he had been given. As I approached his bed to introduce myself, he was in so much agony that he could not converse with me. He thrashed about in constant motion. I said to him, "Let me see if we can relieve the pain and let you have some rest. Then I can come back and talk with you later." I moved in close to him and started to use the "therapeutic touch" by moving both of my hands around his head and down over his body. I moved back and forth - back and forth for about fifteen seconds...and he was out like a light.

He went into a deep sleep. At that moment his doctor entered the room and I attempted to explain to him what I had just done. "Doctor, I've just given him a little prayer therapy." The physician ignored me completely. I could not believe it. He did not even ask me what I had done, even though he had been unable to relieve this young man's pain previously. I thought he would at least want to know if I did something he could use in his practice. Not so. Instead, he tried to wake up his patient and when he finally got him to open his eyes, all he said was, "I'll get you something to help you to sleep." However, before he could give him any medication, the young man went back into his deep slumber and continued to sleep for the next ten hours. When he did awaken not only was his pain gone, his condition was healed. He was released from the hospital on the following day.

The rude treatment I received from that doctor was similar to that received by Dr. Bernie Siegel of Yale University, when he shared his new insights on the treatment of cancer patients, treatments which called for a more personal approach to patients on the part of doctors. He described it in *Love, Medicine & Miracles.*

"I thought I was learning brand-new things that would revolutionize the practice of medicine overnight. I wrote a few articles about these discoveries, but the medical journals returned them. The editors said the subject matter was interesting but advised me to submit them to psychology journals...Next I tried presenting my experiences at medical meetings. The response was hard nosed skepticism, if not outright scorn."[2]

Bernie Siegel was not to be denied his day in court. He has persisted in teaching his views and now support has been coming his way. When I attended one of his seminars, I was impressed to hear a medical doctor speak of the importance of love in the treatment of the sick. He was saying the very things I was saying in my workshops. I related to him easily as a fellow colleague in the service of God and people

I believe that Dolores Krieger has rendered a wonderful service in discovering the *therapeutic touch* and making it available to us. She has offered it as a useful tool for those in her nursing profession. To me, as I use it, it becomes a part of my healing ministry as a variation of the *laying on of hands*. When I *center in* I know that I am praying. As I use it, I feel led by the Spirit. Though I use the *therapeutic touch* frequently I still find the older method useful. I must say the new technique has given me the opportunity for a more versatile way of ministering to the sick. As I move my hands over their heads as they are sitting up in bed, I ask them to experience it as "showers of blessings". Almost without fail, they feel more relaxed and free from anxiety and as such are more receptive to being healed. If pain is present, it often disappears as I am offering them the *therapeutic touch.*

The energy force is real and can often be felt by others in the room. I remember once giving a demonstration of this method and had a volunteer between me and the workshop participants. Not only did the people in the audience feel the energy, but my volunteer received a healing in his hands, though I was not aware that he had a problem.

Dr. Krieger speaks of soothing a crying baby. I have done that many times with the *therapeutic touch,* including one baby who was itching with a serious case of allergy to food. Benjamin was the baby and he not only liked the feeling of the touch, but went home from the healing service to the first good night's sleep in his young life. In time, with more therapeutic touch treatment, the guidance of a good physician and great loving care at home, he was brought to health again.
One time I was on a plane getting ready to take off, when

I heard a child crying out of control in the back of the plane. He was about a year old and had a strong, loud, voice. I think my move was partly self-serving when I left my seat and worked my way back to the young mother with her upset child. Realizing that she did not know me and perhaps might even think it presumptuous on my part, I felt a bit awkward approaching her.

"Hi, I'm not sure it will work...uh, but I think I may be able to calm your child...oh, another thing - if this does work, he's apt to stay asleep quite a while." I thought I had better warn her about that, for on a previous occasion, when I calmed down my associate's baby, Adam, he accommodated us by sleeping about fourteen hours. That sort of worried his mother, Lynn, but when he awakened, full of pep, I was very relieved as well.

The young mother on the plane was so desperate that she readily accepted my offer for help. While we waited there for takeoff I went into my therapeutic touch routine, wafting my hands around him, as the passengers looked on curious, but hoping it would work. I was there only a short time when the attendant asked me to return to my seat. The baby continued to cry until I reached my seat and then ... silence. He remained in a deep sleep for about two hours and finally woke up, making happy sounds for the remainder of the trip home.

I am thankful to Dolores Krieger for having the courage to offer this new approach to her nursing students at New York University and for writing her book, The Therapeutic Touch. I am grateful to this Professor of Nursing for bringing this healing technique to our attention. I am convinced that it is an excellent alternative to other kinds of mental and spiritual therapy being used today in the treatment of the sick.

Chapter 9

Touch for the Dying

Touch for the dying is often glossed over in books on the subject of healing, primarily because healers are dedicated to keeping people from dying. Doctors will do in the hope that tomorrow they may find a cure. As a result we have patients on artificial systems of life-support while they remain in a coma for months or years, as in the case of Karen Ann Quinlan.

There are some persons in spiritual healing that will put up a fierce resistance when the one for whom they have been praying says he/she wants to die. I sensed irritation and anger on the part of some when I told them that my wife, Joan, had made peace with the Lord and was ready to die. It did not matter to them that she had outlived the predicted time of her death by approximately three years...that during those remaining years she had been free from pain and had been given the energy to live a full and productive life - and that she had packed into those final three years a lifetime of ministry to others. All they could see was that she was dying even after they had prayed for her all that time. How dare she? Agnes Sanford shared with me that the same thing had happened in the case of her dying husband, Edgar. She said, "I really believe that he was kept here long past his appointed time by the prayers of so many of our friends who simply could not let him go."

I received some strange requests. From a distant city, a group unknown to us, had requested her picture so they could pray over it so that she might recover. The request came after Joan had made her peace with the Lord and she felt that they were putting pressure on her to accept her healing - as though it was all up to her. Someone else gave us a unique type of rosary, which if used according to specific directions, could keep her from dying.

"What do they want from me?" Jo said to me as tears filled her eyes. "I thought I had handled this sickness all right...gee, Mal, you told me it was all right for me to stop fighting...I'm tired and ready to begin a new life - in fact I'm looking forward to it. Mal, what else do I have to do?"

It is true that she was ready. Just the day before she had visited with a friend, a Sister from the convent at the nearby Carmel Mission. With great joy and anticipation they talked about the adventure that lay before her, the greatest rip of her life. They were both excited about it. You see, to a Christian who believes in the living Christ, death should not be the dreaded specter that it often is, but an open door to a new exciting experience in your future.

Two weeks before her death she had written a letter for me to share with all her friends in which she said, "These three years have been the most meaningful ones to me in my whole life - and I hope that this applies to others with whom I've shared Christ's life within my life...Do not mourn my leaving - but rather rejoice with me that I go to see Him face to face. See you in heaven!"

About the same time she had written the letter she also had written down her requests for her funeral, asking that our bishop, Kilmer Myers, celebrate the Eucharist and then listed a choice of hymns to be sung at the service.

She had fun picking out some of her favorite items of jewelry and called my daughters and her special friends, giving each one the particular pin or bracelet she wanted that person to have. She even gave me her cat, an independent Siamese, named Tashia, who had shown no attraction to me - in fact, she ignored me. Jo had a special way with animals. She talked to them and believed that they understood her. I had my doubts, but there were times when I came close to becoming a believer as in the times she would call out to the birds, "I see you !" and they would come swooping down to her window.

The story of Tashia was such an experience. Tashia was a Siamese cat who was given to us by a friend who had to leave town. Immediately, she took over the house, quickly intimidating the two older cats who lived with us. One was my cat, Middie, so named because she was black as midnight. As Joan was tying together all the loose ends of her life she did not forget Tashia. Since Jo had been resting in bed a lot, Tashia was a constant companion, completely devoted to her human friend. She simply tolerated me. Because of that my wife felt that she should do something to pave the way for our future together, Tashia's and mine.

"Mal, I've been talking with Tashia." In my mind I thought, "Oh, now what?" She continued, " I told her that I was going to be leaving and that she was going to have to change her attitude about you." "That's for sure," I countered. She went on, " No, I'm serious about this ! I let her know that you are really a nice

103

person and that she is going to have to be yours from now on." "That's good," I said but could not imagine what was going to happen next.

At that point Joan said to Tashia, "You're his cat now." Jo had taught Tashia to leap up into her arms on a command. Right after she had spoken those words to the cat, Tashia sat up, got down from the bed, approached me and leaped into my arms. Jo squealed with delight as I stood there in amazement. From that time on Tashia was my cat and my old friend Middie seemed to understand as the Siamese intruder insisted on taking over her favored place in my life. Tashia turned out to be a great comfort to me after Joan had died.

In reading the book, Healing the Dying [1] by my friends, Matt and Denny Linn along with their cousin, Sister Mary Jane Linn, C.S.J., I was struck with the similarity between Mary Jane's recommendations for dealing with the dying and Joan's actions in making her final preparations. In the Preface to the book, Dennis Linn went over Sister Mary Jane's final days and in many ways they paralleled those of Joan. Mary Jane died in a motor accident about a month before their book was published. She had an uncanny desire to go to be with Jesus and to continue to assist her cousins, Denny and Matt, in their ministry from "the other side". She too had prepared her funeral liturgy and left instructions on who was to receive those few items listed as her possessions. As Joan had written her letter, Mary Jane had written her book and left the following note. "If you want to see me you had better hurry up. I think of God and I know that He is going to meet me."

When I read those words I thought of Jo's final

words and realized that the similarities existed because both of these loving souls had come to know Jesus in a very personal way. They were kindred spirits because they truly were "kin" in the family of the church. Each one had felt that she had finished that which was most important in life and now could look forward to a new life of expanded opportunities in Christ's heavenly kingdom. Each was eager to see him face to face.

I was privileged to be present when Jesus came for Joan. She woke me at 4:00 a.m. with the words, "This is the day ! I know it. We need to be up early for there are things to do." It was Wednesday in Holy Week and I was scheduled to be the speaker at the Three Hour Service on Good Friday in my friend, Harvey Buck's church. I had services scheduled for Maundy Thursday, Holy Saturday (I didn't know that one was to be Joan's "Mass of the Resurrection") and of course, there were the Easter celebrations coming up. When I thought of things to do I thought of all my preparations for the days ahead in the church. Joan was thinking of preparations for a new job in heaven. I knew that she was very weak, but I really did not know that this was to be the day that Jesus was to come.

During that day she stayed in bed, while I worked in my home office across the hall. Her mother was in the room with her by her bedside. Every once in a while I would drop into the room to see how she was doing. About one o'clock in the afternoon she called for me and I quickly left my paper work and dashed to her side. She was very weak and I could hardly hear her voice.

"Honey,," she said, "Could you make us some 'Old Fashions'?" I couldn't believe my ears, "Old Fashions?" That had been our drink on special occasions throughout our married life, those times like anniversaries when we had gone "out on the town" to celebrate. I was surprised at her request because she had been able to sip only small amounts of water throughout the day.

I said, "You'll never be able to handle it," and she returned with, "Just make some small ones for a toast." I went off to the kitchen and found some little glasses for liqueurs and made the diminutive "old fashions", each with a tiny piece of cherry and an orange.

She was delighted when she saw my creations. "Just perfect!" she said as she took the small glass in her hand. "Here's to us ! Thanks, Mal, for a wonderful life!" "Here's to us," I repeated, "and I thank you too for everything." We sipped our drinks together and I kissed her gently on the lips. She said, "That was nice, Mal, thanks," and she slipped off to sleep.

An hour and a half had passed when she called for me again. "I think the time is getting close...come sit by my side and hold my hand." Touch had played a large part in my life with Joan. We were lovers as well as mates and we were expressive with one another in our daily lives, with much touching, hugging and holding of hands. Throughout her illness my healing touch had been her principal relief from pain. Whenever she was hurting in a part of her body I could take the pain away by placing my hand on her. My hand would rest there lightly until she gave me the word that everything was all right again. In her final days there was much touching by all of us in the household. Her mother was present to love her. My mother, an R.N., was there to sooth her head as she had soothed mine so many times as a child. And I was there to give my loving touch.

The look of death on the face of a dying person is not always pleasant to behold, though there are exceptions. That is all the more reason for us to minister to them in a loving way. Often the seriously ill are apprehensive and need assurance. Having a hand to hold can be a *healing touch* for the dying. Other forms of touch for the dying are anointing and the *laying on of hands* with prayer which help to take away fear and bring peace into that room. As you offer your touch to the dying, you are being Jesus for that person and your touch becomes as his to the patient. He/she feels the hands and presence of Jesus through your ministry.

In our time the hospice movement has been a blessing to those facing death. Books like *On Death and Dying* [2] by Elizabeth Kubler-Ross have opened our eyes concerning the dying process. Her five stages that the terminally ill go through, namely, denial, anger, bargaining, depression and acceptance have served as the guidelines to help people come to grips with their impending death. With the emergence of attitudinal healing centers and such programs as ECaP, a new honesty with the dying is changing the way patients are able to deal with death. Instead of dying as frightened, confused children, they face death as spiritually whole adults. In fact, occasionally when an "exceptional patient" arrives at the point where she is ready to die, she recovers from the illness.

When Joan called me back to her room I had no idea that I would be witnessing one of Christ's promises to us. In the gospel of John, Jesus told what would happen at the close of their lives.

"Set your troubled hearts at rest. Trust in God

always; trust also in me. There are many dwelling places in my Father's house; if it were not so I should have told you; for I am going there on purpose to prepare a place for you. And if I go and prepare a place for you, I shall come again and receive you to myself, so that where I am you may be also" (John 14: 1-4 NEB).

As I sat there holding Joan's hand I quietly prayed in silence. Then suddenly she arose and sat up in bed, taking off the oxygen mask from her face. As I tried to put it back on she said, "No, I hear something...wait..." Then I watched her face as she turned her head towards the foot of our bed. As she gazed in that direction a look of recognition came to her face as she smiled and her eyes lit up with excitement. She appeared transfixed with that expression and I realized that she had left me. To this day I feel certain that it was Jesus that she saw, coming to receive her as he had promised. That memory has given me a different feeling about death. Joan's story has enabled me to comfort others dealing with the death of a loved one.

It is not only the sick person who goes through the experience of death and dying. The family members share in that process. Particularly the mate is affected. For at least three years the thought of Joan's death lurked in the background of all my thoughts. As we went through three Christmas seasons, each time as I put away the ornaments I wondered if we would decorate a tree together again. As I'd say things like, "When we go to our next parish..." she would interrupt with, "Oh, this place is just fine for us," and I would know that her imminent death was on her mind too.

Sometimes in reciting a poem or singing a song that

we had known for years we'd be struck with something it said. As we were riding in our car from Carmel to Big Sur we were happily singing, "For you take the high road and I'll take the low road, and I'll be in Scotland before you, for me and my true love will never meet again" a n d suddenly she broke out in tears and I gave her my right hand as we continued our ride in silence.

Perhaps the worst kind of mental tricks my mind played on me are those that indicated that I was already planning for my future without her. We might be in a supermarket and I would see an attractive lady and I would think, "she's not a bad prospect" and then berate myself for the thought. She outdid me on that. She even called an attractive widow whom we had known and said to her, "my husband would be a fine prospect for you after I go on to better things." When she told me of this I was surprised and embarrassed. Later on, when the lady made contact with me, I couldn't handle it. I am sure that Jo's intuitive direction was excellent, but in my grief I did not know how to react. It was humbling for me to know that my wife loved me so much she could give me to another.

Because our love was so real I felt guilty for those spontaneous thoughts which made me ask myself if I were "writing her off" before the fact. I say these things to give some assurance to others who may have gone through a similar experience. Some of you may still be feeling some sense of remorse about having such ideas or for having failed in some other way. "Maybe if I had taken her to another doctor?" "If we had gone to a healing service maybe she'd be here today." Other memories bring forth guilt feelings such as, "Why didn't I let him buy that boat he wanted so much and why did I nag at him so ?" Unfortunately, that is all in the past.

109

We cannot do anything to help our loved one now but we can and must get on with our own lives.

Prayer for inner healing can help in such cases. You can go back in the mind's eye to a memory and ask Jesus to help reconcile you and your departed mate. In a confession you can express your sorrow for both the real and imagined hurts you afflicted upon your former spouse and receive forgiveness. I say, "imagined", for if we believe them to be real they will have the same negative affect on us as guilt from real offenses. Merely talking these things out with a friend or counselor can help you to sift the tares from the wheat. We feel guilt at the time of a loved one's death for we all let each other down sometimes.

Help is available for the grieving. Some mortuaries are sponsoring group meetings to help people through the grief process. Those who participate in hospice programs start to receive help before the death of a spouse and are better able to avoid the pitfalls and meet the challenge. All of this requires the healing touch for the bereaved as well as the dying. Whenever people gather together with a common need and offer to share each other's burdens they are given help from the Lord. They all receive the healing touch.

Journal writing takes many forms and can be a *healing touch* of sorts to those facing death. My friend, Marjorie, came to our healing service after she had been diagnosed with a serious cancer condition. She had been brought up in the church but had been out of touch for some years. An artist, she had learned the folk lore of Alaska's native people and depicted these stories in her paintings. Her identification with the native people and their traditions created some confusion in her mind about Jesus. Most of the Indian and Eskimo people of Alaska are now Christian, though the legends of their culture live on through their stories and dances and art. After coming to our healing services she realized that she did not know Jesus as we seemed to know him. The notes she made showed a gradual development in her faith, particularly her relationship with Jesus as her notes progressed. In journal writing, a person asks a question of God and then writes the answer which comes to him from his inner mind as inspired writing. Through that process Marjorie was given a healing touch as she worked her way through the following questions and answers.

MARG: "Dear God, I'm so tired and worn out and discouraged. What should I do?"

GOD: "Rest, rest, my child. I am here with you now".

MARG: "Dear God, please, oh Lord, help me to have serenity. Please, oh Lord, help my stomach to feel better, and Lord, I don't know what to do about this confusion of religious ideas I'm getting. What should I do"?

GOD: "Just rest, my child, do nothing right now".

MARG: "Should I try to know Jesus ? He seems foreign to me"..

At this point we have a break in her writing. When Marjorie returns to her writing it is apparent that she has had a religious experience. Her writing continues but not

111

with a question but with a description of her experiences and an expression of her thanks.

MARG: "Dear Lord: Thank you so much that when I asked for help, I got it - all sorts of help, Dr. Webb and tranquilizers and today BAPTISM IN THE HOLY SPIRIT ..... at least I think so. My spirit is filled with joy and very haltingly, the ability to speak in tongues. What a joyful experience ! Thank you Lord for the healing group and its blessing. Thank you for the blessing of my raven - that was special ! That rang right... and Oh God, I want to pray as well as Father Miner. Then will you tell me (or show me) why people pray to Jesus. Will you do that, Father"?

GOD: "Yes, my child, be open and listening and I will tell you".

MARG: "Oh Lord, I reject the diagnosis of my disease and I thank you for healing... and please, oh Lord, help me to put it into my unconscious mind that I am going to get well. I now feel ready to accept the risk of disappointment. Thank you, oh Lord, for the Gifts of the Spirit ! and oh Lord, if the fear comes back, send me Jesus to grapple with it and defeat it".

Through her journal writing Marjorie had found a Jesus to whom she could relate. She continued to come to our healing services which she felt gave her strength to cope with her illness. When she first appeared she was frightened and confused, but as time went on she became more secure in her faith and began offering her "healing touch" to others. As she weakened some of the members of the prayer group kept in touch and visited with her in her home. When she was in the hospital

112

close to death her husband, Gene, called me to her side. She was very upset and somewhat irrational when I arrived. I gave her a healing blessing using the therapeutic touch method which relaxed her immediately. The blessing did not heal her but served as a reprieve in which she was restored temporarily, giving her time to say her "good-byes" before going to sleep peacefully in the Lord. Following her death Gene discovered these notes and others which revealed that Marjorie had developed a close relationship with her God. In her case she had found help from the love of her husband, Gene and her children, from her physician who gave her medical advice and chemotherapy, from the Order of St. Luke group at the church and their prayer ministry and from corresponding with God through journal writing. Her help came from different people at different times but in each instance her Lord was behind it all giving his *healing touch*.

Touch for the dying is a ministry of its own. The Tibetan Buddhist writer, Sogyal Rinpoche, chides us in the Western world for not spending adequate time with this subject in his book, *The Tibetan Book of Living and Dying* This book offers much that is helpful to anyone working with the dying. Even when people are not healed in the body we feel that they can be healed in mind and spirit. With hope for a new life with God, which offers opportunities for growth and service, the spiritual healing is perhaps the most important of all. Recognizing that a person is probably dying does not mean the abdication of hope for physical healing. As I often say as I visit with the family of a sick person, "When I pray to God I ask for 'the works'...and then thank him for whatever we get." That means that sometimes our healing touch makes the patient well again. Other times it calms his spirit as a "touch for the dying" that helps him to die with dignity and peace.

Chapter 10

Disclaimers of Touch

In spite of what appears to be overwhelming evidence of the blessings of touch in its many forms, there are always disclaimers who are ready to take issue with many of the techniques I have discussed. Those who take a literal view of the Bible believe that only healing in the name of Jesus Christ is valid. However, a look around the world will show us that healing through mental and spiritual methods is found in many world religions and has been successfully practiced by persons not subscribing to any creed. The critics who are most apt to find fault are those who look at the world as essentially evil. True, it often appears that there is an evil force at work in the world in the minds of men. The Bible states that when God made the world he was satisfied that it was good. He endowed all living things with natural gifts which would enable them to cope with the environment and survive. Chop off a branch of a tree and if it is strong and healthy, it will survive. Chop off the tail of a lizard and it will grow a new one. The animals have been given instinctive abilities to let them know what to do when they are sick or injured. Human beings have received those gifts as well and through using their minds, they have learned many other ways to heal the sick.

In each primitive culture there rose up men or women who were known as "shamans". In such a society all tasks were defined according to sex with the exception of one. The role of healer could be either male or female.

That was due to the fact that healers were appointed from on high, from the spirit world. As they practiced the art of healing, shamans would derive their power from within their unconscious minds. That is why some Christians are concerned when we use techniques which involve our *going within.*

However, it was Jesus, himself, who told us that we would find the kingdom of heaven within. When a Christian healer uses his/her intuitive resources, he/she is first asking that the Holy Spirit enter in to guide in that process. Jesus promised that the Spirit would be with us as a guide and as the one who would empower us to heal the sick. True, when we go within, we are using methods similar to those used by healers since the dawn of civilization, but that does not mean that we still believe as they did. Our present faith took years to come to fruition in the way we know it today. Jesus built on the faith of the prophets through hundreds of years. His ministry was the fulfillment of the Law as it had been presented to Moses and the prophets. We who have come to know Jesus follow in his way and make our judgments on the basis of his teaching and example. Our faith continues to grow through the inspiration of the Holy Spirit. By opening ourselves to our own unconscious minds, we are also opening ourselves to a direct encounter with the Spirit. That allows us to know God, not only through the experiences of others, but in a deep personal way as well.

John Sanford, the priest-psychologist explains how most people remain insulated from a first-hand encounter with God in his book, *Healing and Wholeness.*

"In the Old Testament we have the original experiences of the prophets in which men like Moses, Isaiah, and Ezekiel were spoken to directly by God. Later these personal experiences were institutionalized into the Judaic religion. In Christianity we have the unique relationship between Jesus and his Heavenly Father, and the immediate religious experiences of the apostles. However, within a few centuries these persona experiences became enshrined in the Christian Church with its tradition, ritual and doctrine. In this way an original, primary religious experience of certain individuals became the secondary religious experience of the masses. Thus most people do not know God, but only hear about Him through the experiences of others, and religious structures that claim to lead people to God may, in fact, serve to keep people from God by shielding them from, their own experience with the numinous."[1]

Conservative Christians have discouraged going within as a means of having a personal religious experience primarily because it has been a method used by witch doctors. Shamans use a method of altering their state of consciousness at will, arriving at a source of knowledge previously not known to them. They do this by entering into the area of the unconscious mind, the vast storehouse of memories and source of our dreams. Some of these practices, such as the use of the imagination, come to us naturally. We go through a period in our childhood, when we use the imaginary world for our growth and development. That right brain activity is usually discouraged by our adult teachers, our parents and our peers and eventually we scarcely use our imagination at all.

In recent years there has been a emphasis on the

activities of the right brain as a resource for inspiration as well as healing. Holistic medicine, psychotherapy, meditation, biofeedback, possibility thinking and hypnosis have all appeared under Christian auspices. Some Christians see these methods as products of "New Age" thinking and believe they pose a threat to the Christian religion. Many of those who call themselves "New-agers" are dropouts from the traditional churches. They are trying something different because what they had was not working for them. "New Age " is not an organized religion. Its adherents are those who are seeking new ways of developing their own spirituality, so it often seems to be a hodge-podge of practices. Essentially they are seekers and as a result end up exploring whatever teachings give meaning to their lives. You may not agree with them they don't even agree with each other, but many of these folk are using their talents in different kinds of service to others - massage, different forms of hands on healing for which they are criticized. I believe that God can use us all.

The use of visualization in healing has been assailed by some as dangerous. All of us use some kinds of visualization normally. When lovers are absent from one another, they picture their beloved in their mind's eye. We may employ visualization as an aid to worship. That is how many of us become closer to Jesus. We picture him when we pray. Even when we look upon a crucifix or a painting of our Lord we are being helped by the visualization of the artist who created the art work. We can imagine him by our bedside when we are sick. We can see him in our room when we are lonely. Using our imagination, we can have him walk back with us in time to some painful experience and have him heal that memory now. Thus we can have a personal

118

encounter with our Lord.

The use of visualization for healing purposes has been highly successful as a technique to promote inner healing. Visualization has been criticized by some because non Christian medicine men or shamans also used that concept. The shamans were very important persons within their cultures. Like all human beings, some were good and emphasized the positive aspects of life and health. Others used their gifts to control people. Those healers were very gifted as herbalists and knew which plants were helpful in the treatment of disease. There is evidence to show that they were skillful in counseling, being the psychiatrists of their times. The book, The Clan of the Cave Bear,[2] offers some helpful insights as to how these persons performed in their primitive societies. Merely because other human beings used practices such as visualization does not automatically make those practices wrong. When we were created we were given a variety of gifts to help us cope with life. Some of those gifts were universal, long before Christianity or any of the other great world religions known today. Some of the spiritual gifts of human beings are natural for all of us, as we are all children of God, made in his image. Though we may not be aware of it, we are all spiritual beings, though we often tend to rely solely on our minds and bodies. When those outside the Church use spiritual means to heal the sick some Christians insist on attributing those healings to the devil. If it is not in the name of Jesus, it must be of the evil one. Yet those same persons are willing to receive healing from doctors who heal through natural means such as surgery and pills.

I believe that the root of the criticism of spiritual healers by conservative Christians is their narrow view of the Bible. In fact, all of their arguments hinge on a very literal interpretation of Holy Scripture. They seem afraid to trust human beings to use the very resources of body, mind and spirit that were given to us by our Creator. I agree with them that we should proceed with caution in those areas. We do have some justification in not trusting in some practices just because others are using them. We should learn what others have experienced and evaluate their results before we adopt methods that are new to us. We should be secure in our faith and in harmony with our Lord as we venture within. I personally subscribe an old Anglican tradition which points to a threefold source for our knowledge of God: the authority of the Bible, the experience of the Church and Reason. We need to utilize more than one source to learn the truth about God. We can turn to the Holy Scriptures as inspired writings, where the truth of God can be found. That is different from the fundamentalist position which claims that the entire Bible is the literal Word of God where every word in every book is inspired truth. I believe that we can find the Word of God in the Bible, but it is also true that we can learn a lot about God from reading other inspired writings and observing our world and the universe.

In addition to that, we have the history and authority of the Church itself, which has been making an effort to follow the guidance of the Holy Spirit through the ages. We have the writings of the Church Fathers and even today we look for God's revealed word as he inspires writers in many fields of learning. We read and listen and digest this information with the help of our minds, which also are a gift from our creator God to us. I'm not speaking of the minds of men versus the mind of God. I am speaking of the minds of men being inspired by the Spirit of God. Once the guidance has come from the Holy Spirit we are often required to use our minds in order to carry out God's will. Some Christians have a problem trusting in the natural gifts we have received from our creator.

Jews, Moslems and Christians have all been "people of the Book" - the Old Testament, the Koran and the Bible. Other religions also have sacred writings, believed by them to be the only truth of God. We must not weigh the value of everything by the use of our scriptures alone. We must face the fact that none of us has the whole truth. No matter what we read, each of us puts his/her own interpretation on the words. There are things I write or say that you will not be able to accept. The truth for each of us is the combined reading and experience common only to ourselves. However, we find that we can and do agree with others who have been a part of our learning experience. As Christians we share with the Jews in much of their belief and practice. That is true to a certain extent with Islamic believers and similarities to our beliefs can be found in other religions of the world. Since I came to live in Hawaii I have come to know Buddhists, both lay persons and Priests. I have worked with some of these ministers as a member of our local hospital's Chaplaincy Program. I have felt a kinship to them and their people and no longer look at them as "pagans", but rather as brothers and sisters in the family of mankind. When we try, we see that we agree with others in many ways. With that kind of vision we can have some hope for the world. Because we are secure in our own faith does not mean that God does not care for or listen to the prayers of his other children. We may be happy that we have a revelation of

God that is good, so good that we feel that it is "the true faith". Others may feel that they have "the true faith" and trust in the revelation they believe has been given to them. I cannot help but believe that the Lord who said, "I have come that they might have life, and that they might have it more abundantly" (John 10:10 KJV), offered that for all of his people. If God is truly concerned with all of his people, then surely, he will find a way to reach all of them with his love and forgiveness and hope.

Yes, there are disclaimers, who are out there in the world, ready to put down any good idea that does not fit their definition of the truth. Unfortunately, some of the very ones who oppose you share your concerns about human need and really should be your allies in the service of others. I mentioned previously how Dr. Bernie Siegel, in his book, *Love, Medicine & Miracles,* tells of his frustration with his fellow physicians, who were not willing to consider trying some of his methods, which seemed far out to them. Basically, his methods fit well with those of us in healing ministries. Essentially, he is saying that we should be personal with those we seek to help. We must not be afraid to express our feelings, including our love and concern, but also in some instances, our disagreement and our anger. What he suggests should not be that difficult to achieve, but many in medicine are married to their more impersonal ways, which protect them from any emotional involvement with their patients.

Within the churches there is a similar attitude towards those who are out in front with a healing ministry. Though your healing touch, your gifts of intuition and your right brain functions are normal and natural, there are those who will look upon them as different or impractical. If you have the ability to take away someone's pain with a touch but do not use that gift because of criticism or the fear that you might look foolish, some suffering will continue unnecessarily because you failed to act. Remember, that Paul said, We are fools for Christ's sake".

There will always be disclaimers. Often they are sincere persons, who love the Lord as you love the Lord. Others will criticize merely to tear down and destroy. Some will say that "those things are all right for you, but I don't feel comfortable with your approach." That should be something we can accept. Those who differ from us are not necessarily our adversaries. They are merely making their observations from a different point of view. Some are gifted in theology and doctrine, those who serve primarily as students and teachers of the Holy Scriptures. Some are the contemplatives, who will make their offerings in the area of prayer and meditation. Each of us has his/her own place. However, if you are one of those whom God has called to an active ministry in human service, then do not be discouraged by those who criticize you and others who do not share your interests and goals. Disclaimers are not new. They have always been here to test us and to help us to evaluate our thinking. When we listen carefully to what they are saying and have satisfactorily answered their criticisms, we become stronger then ever.

Chapter 11

Responsibility in Touch

"Go out to the whole world; proclaim the Good News associated with believers: in my name they will cast out devils...they will lay hands on the sick, who will recover" (Mark 16: 16-18 JER).

That is what the "Divine Commission" has to say about healing -"they will cast out devils", all kinds of devils like FEAR and GUILT and HATE among other things and "they will lay hands on the sick who will recover." Those orders were given by Jesus to the Church the last time he met with his disciples. It is incredible to me that so many can read these parting words of the Master and ignore what he had to say about healing. Healing the sick is a responsibility of the Christian Church.

As we read in my chapter on the Jesus Touch, the apostles were quick to emulate their teacher as they began their ministries as healings abounded in the early church. Stories of healing were commonplace during the first three centuries of the church's life, but as empires rose and fell and hardship and suffering became the norm, then a greater emphasis was placed on the life hereafter. Anointing for the sick shifted to anointing as the last sacrament, preparing people for a "happy death". Along with that shift was the shift from love and mercy to penance and redemptive suffering - again to gain a foothold in heaven. Healings only came now and then as verifications of a holy person's sainthood. Other healings were close to magic, particularly if one could possess a fragment from "the true cross" or a piece of cloth, reported to be "the hem of his garment" to help effect a cure. The Dark Ages were desperate times with little hope left in the hearts of men.

In spite of the pessimistic attitude of the church leaders, healings did continue here and there in isolated situations. We know, from looking at the ingredients that produce healing, that healing cannot help but happen when believing people pray for others in a caring way. No doubt many were healed by spiritual means where it was not credited to prayer. That happens today. A loving mother gives totally of herself in caring for her sick child and without even knowing it, gives the laying on of hands and the child is healed. The mother in comforting and loving her child while appealing to God silently in her thoughts has become the agent of healing that has returned her baby to health. Those of you who are reading this book have also been healers when you have reached out and touched someone. You say, "Isn't it just wonderful how you've improved during the time I've been here !" Of course, it's wonderful. You healed your friend and never even knew your part in it. Just think how much better you could do if you became aware of your own "healing touch" and used it with expectancy. My mother was a nurse with healing hands and soothed her patients and gave them hope. Her granddaughters, Linda and Donna also use their hands for healing, but they know that they are using a kind of therapy that works - so they expect more and receive more than my mother did. Yes, healing does go on whether we notice it or not and throughout all the years of the church's life it has been present somewhere. But it is our responsibility to restore it to its position as the cutting edge of Christ's ministry to the world: *TO PREACH THE GOOD NEWS AND HEAL THE SICK.*

As time went on the Good News continued to be preached but the other worldly approach dominated the teaching. Martin Luther turned things around with his direct personal approach to God through faith rather than works. With that came the emphasis on "the priesthood of all believers" which opened the door to active involvement in ministry on the part of lay persons. Now each one of us became responsible to the Lord for seeing that his work was done. The Anglican priest, John Wesley was moved when he witnessed the personal approach of some Moravians in prayer. He saw the need to involve the laity in evangelistic efforts and schooled them with a methodical program of study, worship and prayer which led to their being known as *"Methodists"*. Finding no support from the bishops of his own church, Wesley "laid hands *on"* some devout laymen and without knowing it, created a new Christian body which eventually became known as the Methodist Church. Starting in England they moved to the colonies in America where the Methodist "circuit riders" figured prominently after the revolution. The churches they established seemed to thrive in the informal atmosphere of the frontier. Unknown to most of today's Methodists, Wesley was involved in healing. In his *Journal* John Wesley cited many examples of healing as a result of prayer, a number of these by his own hand.

In spite of these references to healing, the judgment and wrath of God received a more prominent place from the fiery preachers of the reformation churches. The Roman Catholic Church kept its people under its domination as did the Calvinists and the Puritans. Religion was deadly serious and there was not much room for an emphasis on the love of God or healing. Even the healing liturgies dealt mostly with the sinfulness of man, giving the dying person an ample chance to repent for his sins, thought by many to be the cause of his illness.

With the vacuum created by the neglect of healing in the traditional churches, healing by spiritual means came to the public's attention through Mary Baker Eddy approximately a hundred years ago. As a sick person she went for help to a Phineas P. Quimby, who taught that all illnesses were due to errors of thought and that healing would result if only a person could know right thinking. It was some time later that she received her healing, while she was alone, reading the Bible. In 1878 she organized the Christian Science Church, based on the premise that a good and perfect God creates only that which is good and that evil and disease are only illusions in people's minds. She remained aloof from the other churches, which she believed were unable to see the truth in the teachings of Jesus. Other New Thought groups such as Religious Science and Unity have developed, sharing many of the same concepts. With their emphasis on the positive and on healing there is no doubt that many have been healed as a result of their efforts.

In his comprehensive work, *Healing and Christianity,* Morton Kelsey marks the early 1900's as the time when a new spirit began to emerge in both medicine and the church. He cites the formation of groups organized to create a better climate between people in religion with those in medicine. In England the Guild of Health was established for that purpose. In the United States, the Order of St. Luke was started by an Episcopal priest, Dr. John Gayner Banks and the Schools of Pastoral Care were developed by Agnes Sanford, who had a great influence on many of us who are active today in the healing ministry. Both the Lambeth Conference of Anglican bishops and Vatican II made positive pronouncements concerning the rightful place of healing in the church. The Roman Catholic Church made a statement which restored anointing to its place as a healing sacrament, not only for those who are dying, as in "Extreme Unction", but also as a healing ministration as well.

Finally, in our time we have had the Renewal Movement with its Pentecostal influence on the mainline churches, emphasizing lay ministry and the Gifts of the Spirit. We have seen evidence of a rebirth of healing through this movement which has brought an apostolic flavor back into the churches. Today, even in the formal, liturgical churches, there are prayer groups and healing masses and happy singing of "renewal songs". It is no longer strange to hear people speaking in tongues, uttering prophecies and otherwise demonstrating Gifts of the Spirit noted in the Book of Acts. The Christian churches of today are beginning to accept the responsibility given to them in The Divine Commission.

The first "responsibility in touch" was given to the Church by Jesus as he sent his disciples forth into the world to preach the Good News and to heal the sick. In practice the ones who must accept responsibility are those persons who have been called to the healing ministry. Healing was ignored in the churches so many years that the idea of pastors serving as healers still seems foreign to most people. When you bring in the idea of lay persons offering healing prayer therapy to those who are ill, medical people really begin to show some concern.

The credibility of both clergy and lay persons as therapists in healing is difficult to establish. At a church service a person may receive "the baptism of the Holy Spirit" and become convinced of his/her gift of healing. That is all the knowledge and authority some persons need to launch out as "healers" praying for the sick wherever they may find them. Experience has shown us that such persons may indeed be able to lay hands on the sick with excellent results. Unfortunately, that does not apply to everyone who feels called to a ministry of healing.

As we become more involved in that type of service we need to become aware of some pitfalls along the way. One danger is the danger of making our involvement in healing our own Ego trip. The first attempts at healing, whether they be trying out the therapeutic touch or joining in prayer with others at a healing service are exciting when your patient is improved or healed. There is a temptation for you to see that special power as yours alone and forget to give credit to the real source of power. When your ministry is basically for your own satisfaction the patient and his/her needs becomes secondary. The problem is not new. There are many physicians who fall prey to the same Ego need.

However, in order to convince others of the reality of spiritual healing you need to share your success stories and in doing so, some may accuse you of blowing your own horn. As long as you know that you are not on an Ego trip is all that matters. If you begin to blame the patient for not getting well after your prayer therapy you probably need to examine your motives.

The story of finding a dying woman in the hospital who had been abandoned by her church because she had not "claimed her healing" lets us know how far religious people can get away from their calling to serve others. Fortunately my friend, Jim found that lost soul and we were able to bring Christ's love and touch to her during her final days. Where were those Christians who had left her to die alone ? Maybe they became frustrated when they offered all they had and nothing worked. Who knows?

It is true that some of the ones we try to help can be difficult and will not cooperate with us. Some of them complain constantly and after awhile their negativity may rub off on you. However, if you are to be responsible in your personal healing ministry you need to have patience with your problem cases. There are times when your feelings may be hurt when your patient rejects your ministrations. In spite of that you need to be able to stand by that sick person, even when you do not seem to be appreciated. There are times when all you can do is to remain there and pray in silence. Often when it is all over and the patient has made it through the crisis he/she will thank you for all you have done, even though you think your contribution was of little value.

Healing the sick is usually a shared experience. When we see a person healed by your very touch it is easy to forget all of the others who may have had a part in that healing. A man came to our healing service, complaining of stomach cramps and stress. I laid hands on him for healing and he left without saying anything. He returned twice more and following the third time he received prayer he said, "I was healed the first night I came here...I wanted to be sure it was going to work before I said anything - and now I'm sure !" Because of that healing experience that man was able to convince his own clergyman to begin having healing services in their church. I told this story to demonstrate how we share in a healing with other therapists. After his healing I found out that the patient had been in counseling therapy for some time with my colleague, Lee Stratman. At a certain point Lee had said, "I think we've talked this over enough...now why don't you go to Malcolm's healing service and see if that will help." You see, the healing which appeared to be an instant healing that first evening had begun with Lee's first counseling session.

Whenever you visit a patient in the hospital you know that he/she has been receiving treatment from a physician, usually involving medicine or surgery. Some of those sick persons are receiving physical therapy as well. Many persons become involved in a person's healing process. You may think that you alone have just given the miraculous touch when a sick person suddenly is restored after your prayer therapy. It is important to remember how many others have most likely shared in that process. You see, God is behind all healing. He is there with the surgeon, guiding his hand. He is with the nurse as she massages the person's back or applies the therapeutic touch. His presence is in the midst of those bands of "exceptional" patients working together to become survivors. And you are grateful to know he is with you when you apply your own healing touch. All of us in healing are in his service for it is by his grace that we heal.

That is why we must be sensitive to the hospital professionals when we go there to offer our healing gifts. Part of our responsibility is to know hospital procedure and follow the rules. Some hospitals offer training for those who wish to visit the sick. When I lived in Anchorage, that service was offered by Providence Hospital, a Roman Catholic institution and many of the members of our Order of St. Luke took the course. That is one way lay persons can gain credibility in their ministries as hospital visitors, to take a course and be certified by that hospital. Clinical training is available for most students in theological schools and is required for pastors desiring work as hospital chaplains. Taking such a course will not teach you to be a healer - God will give you those gifts but it will help you to cooperate with the other workers in the healing arts, the doctors, the nurses, and those others who staff our healing centers.

Most of us involved with a healing ministry are members of a church or an organization dedicated to healing. In this chapter we are discussing "Responsibilities in Touch", the Church's responsibility to carry out the Divine Commission and our responsibilities to the patient and the healing center or hospital and finally to our church or the support group we represent. As a teenager on my way to a party or a school event my mother used to say to me as I was about to leave, "Remember who you are and whom you represent," and I'd answer, "Yep," as I slammed the door and went on my way. As we present ourselves to the sick person we are putting our own reputation on the line but we also represent our organization. The good or bad that we do reflects back on our organization but also reflects on all of our fellow workers in the healing ministry. We must never take advantage of the sick person's captive status to make our visitation a time for a sermon. Make yourself available to him/her but don't be pushy. Do not use that time as an opportunity to convert him/her to your particular program or creed. Remember, you are a guest in that room, for the hospital is the patient's temporary home, so we must act accordingly. Those of us who are there responding to the Lord's command must never forget that they represent him as well. We must be Jesus for those who need him. Your witness will be the way others judge your ministry - the doctors and nurses, the family and friends of the one who is ill and the patient him/herself. Last but not least, "Remember who you are and whom you represent" If you are going to be Jesus for somebody, play your part well.

Chapter 12

Putting Touch to Use

"You are the very person we need! We have a friend who is very sick...paralyzed and can't walk. Would you be willing to go to the hospital and give her the "laying on of hands" for healing?"

My friend, Howard Park, had just recently signed up as an Associate Member of the Order of St. Luke the Physician. He had spent some time at our OSL services, observing us as we prayed for the sick with the "laying on of hands", but he had not actively participated in that. He had approved of what we were doing, but had been reluctant to accept a leadership role in our local chapter. Now he found himself in a new location far from our group, and someone needed help. There was no one to call upon. What was he to do?

Soon after he had arrived he had offered his services to a center providing help for those with alcoholic problems. Good volunteers are hard to find and Howard seemed like a gift from God. He knew what he was doing and did not seem to mind putting in hours at the center. Curious about this caring person, the director, whose name was Karen, sought more information from him.

"You have an unusual way with people. You really seem to care! Are you some kind of a minister?" and receiving no reply to that, she continued, "You're different... you sure you aren't involved with some kind of ministry?"

"No," he hesitated, and remembering his connection with us, he ventured, "Well, I do belong to the Order of St. Luke...uh, it's an organization involved with healing".
That is when she responded with such enthusiasm saying to him, "You are the very person we need", and followed this up with a request for him to go to the hospital and offer some healing prayer.

You can imagine how he felt. With no real experience praying for the sick he was being asked to go to the front line. He had admitted to being a member of this healing order and now they were expecting something special from him. He was hoping that they would forget this, but that was in vain. Other friends of the sick person followed up on that request and asked him to give their friend the laying on of hands. He agreed to go, but wondered it it was smart of him to mention his involvement with the Order of St. Luke.

"Now, what have I got myself into," he thought as he headed for the hospital. "Maybe I should have involved myself more at the healing services...God help me to do this thing right." He was somewhat unnerved as they entered the hospital room, where he was introduced as a "healer".

"Hey, I'm just one of you...nothing special about me. In fact, I'm going to need you to join with me on the prayer. I hope you'll be willing to help me."

That was good thinking on Howard's part, bringing in others to share in that effort. He was counting on the strength in numbers, for he had seen that work at the OSL meetings. By the time they arrived at the hospital the support group had increased in size, overflowing the small room where the patient lay immobile. Her eyes lit up when she saw them enter.

Karen explained to her what was happening, that they had brought this man from the Order of St. Luke to offer a healing prayer. As they gathered around the bed of their friend, Howard asked them to join hands as he prayed. Nervously, he approached the patient but as he touched her on the head he spoke with authority, "In the name of Jesus Christ be healed".

At that very moment, everyone in the room felt a charge of energy go through them - and no one was more amazed than Howard. What he did not know was that in taking this step of faith, he began a process which would lead him, not only into an active role in the Order of St. Luke, but eventually into the full time ministry of the Church. In the months that followed he became involved with a local church, received the rite of confirmation and became a serious student of theology. In time the former engineer who thought he had retired, attended seminary and eventually was ordained as a priest in the Episcopal Church. I had the joyful privilege of installing him as a chaplain in the Order of St. Luke.

The patient was uplifted and encouraged by that experience. There was a drastic improvement in her condition following their visit. She was eventually given back the use of her limbs and was released from the hospital, walking. The people in that community felt certain that they had found a friend with the gift of healing. Howard was relieved and thankful that he was not alone on his first mission of healing.

While I was on a teaching mission with the Eskimos of Point Hope, Alaska, I was asked by the native priest to go with him to the home of a parishioner confined to her bed. As we walked towards her house I noticed that we were being joined by others along our route. When we arrived at the modest dwelling we were accompanied by an entourage of friends and relatives who had come to pray with us. There were more people than chairs, so most of the people sat on the floor. Father Oktolik walked with me to the lady's bedside and said to her, "Father Miner, he is healing priest who come here to teach us about healing...he anoint you now and make you well." The dear lady smiled at me as he told her why I was there. Her body was wasted away, she was just skin and bones but her spirit radiated through that smile.

I took the vial of oil from the priest and anointed her and prayed for her healing and then prepared to leave. At that point I realized that there was more to come. One by one, each person in that room offered a prayer for their sick friend in their native language. The love and concern that poured from their hearts was very real to me, though I could not understand a word they were saying, with the one exception of "Jesus" which appeared every now and then among the Inuit words. I could sense the presence of God in that room.

I could not help but be impressed with the involvement of those people in that healing ministry. Healing prayer had become a normal way of life for them.

Had my friend, Howard, been a member of their prayer team he would have felt much more at ease when asked to lead in prayer. In that small Arctic congregation no one was allowed to sit in the back seat and observe. However, in our culture there are many more observers than participants when it comes to prayer therapy for healing.

Many of us are like Howard. We have barely put our toes in the waters of the healing ministry. Perhaps we have been attending services and praying from a distance. Maybe it has been our habit to consider prayer therapy something for the professionals or the truly gifted. Perhaps we feel that we do not have the qualifications, or maybe we are fearful or apprehensive. We believe in it as long as someone else is doing it. However, if you suspect that God is calling you to that ministry, you will need to make a decision. Sooner or later you must stop being a spectator or "hearer of the word" only, and step out in faith as Howard did and become a "doer of the word".

There is no doubt that accepting the role of healer can be a frightening experience. Though I had many years in this ministry, I still have times when I am unsure of myself. At those times it seems as though I must shoulder the whole weight of responsibility myself. I feel as though I have been put on the spot. Because I have been teaching others about healing, sometimes I feel that the burden of proof is mine to deliver. That is not good thinking on my part. When the crisis has cleared and I have regained my senses, I know that the Lord is the healer and that as we give him the glory we also give him the responsibility.

We have been talking about the advantages of healing with a prayer group. Sometimes it is easier to deal with a sick person all by yourself. If you call when there are a lot of visitors it is difficult to get the patient's attention. A sick person wants help and usually desires a *healing touch*, so try to find a time to be alone with him or her. That is a time when you and the patient can develop a rapport with each other. If you are new at this, seeing the suffering person will help you to forget your own anxieties and you will be ready to help the best you can.

We are most effective when we accept the role of "being Jesus" for someone in need. He is my model and I try to be to that person the way Jesus would be. In the first place I try to love the sick person and see the good in that person the way Jesus sees the good in each of us. I try to give the patient comfort by telling him/her that I am there to help - that Jesus is there to help. Let the sick person know that you believe in healing and that you think that prayer with the laying on of hands will be helpful.

If the patient is in pain say, "Let's see if we can do something to relieve this pain", and then lay your hands upon the sick person (or maybe you will use the therapeutic touch method) and thank God for what he is now doing for the patient. You will soon be able to know that the sick person is being relieved. His/her face will change and a sense of peace will become obvious as he/she smiles at you. Then you will want to say a "thank you" to God, who has been working through you.

Forget yourself and your fears and concentrate on the needs of the sick person. Then continue to be "Jesus" for that person in his/her need. It may seem presumptuous to be Jesus for someone, but that is exactly what he has asked us to do. Back in the fourth chapter we read of his promise that "they shall lay hands on the sick, and they shall recover" (Mark 16:18 KJV). He really wanted us to take his place in ministering to others.. in

139

fact, it was given as a command: Go and do it.

If you think that you might have healing gifts, but you are not quite sure, try it out where it is easier, with your own family and close friends. As I said earlier, I began using the laying on of hands with my children when they were very young. They accepted my ministrations as natural, and when the healing came, it assured us all that it was good. I told you how my own children became self-assured in ministering to the sick by praying for their pet hamsters and other animals. In another situation I remember my son, Philip, at three years of age, laying hands on a doll to "make him well".

Suppose that you do feel called to a ministry of touch. How do you get involved? Do you go to the nearest hospital and say, "Here I am, ready to heal all you lucky people?" Hardly, for who would listen to you? You need some kind of credibility to be involved in healing, something besides a "call" to that ministry. That is important for you but others will expect you to have some credentials, such as membership in a support group like the Order of St. Luke or that you are an approved lay chaplain for a local church. Unfortunately, there are some persons who act irresponsibly on their own and give us all a bad name.

If you are seriously interested in healing go where something is being done. .Finding others who are involved in ministry can give you some opportunity to see what you can do to help others. Many churches have training for hospital visitation and I have mentioned previously that some hospitals provide courses which certify both the clergy and lay persons in a hospital ministry. Sometimes you will find courses offered at your local colleges on the therapeutic touch.

The Lord calls us to ministry...some he calls to an active role in healing. If you feel you have gifts of healing to offer, you need to get involved. Observing others is good. Sharing with a group in prayer is better. It helps us to know that we are not alone in our endeavors. When we hear the good reports of how others are restored, we become convinced that spiritual healing works. Joining with a prayer group gives us confidence for the time when we shall be by ourselves in a healing situation. Learning through a course of study is good, through reading what others have experienced in their own ministries. However, we must remember that we could never learn to swim merely by observing and reading about swimming. Sooner or later we must get into the water.

Getting into the water will mean different things for different people. Not everyone will want to be involved in the kind of healing ministry I have been describing. So far, this chapter has been concentrating on a certain kind of touch, the *healing touch* used with the sick. However, touch is needed by all of us for our nurture. Remember what I said previously about babies dying for the lack of touch? Merely being free from disease does not mean we are whole. For wholeness we need lots of things, such as another person's respect, appreciation, forgiveness, encouragement, and caring. The way we either give these or deny them to others becomes a touch of sorts. Being kind and appreciative to another is like the touch of a fond embrace. At the other extreme, to fail to notice or appreciate someone amounts to giving them a hurtful touch - a "slap in the face".

We do not need to be mentally ill to suffer from hurts and mental anguish. All of us need the nourishment that comes from touch. That means you and me, our lovers or our mates, our children and friends...all those other folks out there. We may never feel comfortable as healers, but that does not prevent us from using touch with others. One of the phone companies has been advertising on TV with a slogan, "Reach out and touch someone". A friendly phone call certainly can be a warm and nurturing kind of touch. Again, that is something all of us can do.

I began this book discussing how much touch comes into play with the newborns in other cultures. I shared some of my own touch experiences with my own children, the hugging, the holding, the rocking, the rolling, the massaging and the soothing. Yes, those things are needed by all of us and are as important to our well being as the food we eat.

In the midst of all this emphasis on touching I need to throw in a word of caution. There are some among us, who for some unknown reasons cannot stand to be touched. Recently I called upon a young woman who was in a depression. I mentioned that I came by to get acquainted and perhaps, give a healing touch. Just as soon as I said that, she said, "I can't stand being touched anywhere on my body !" I could understand how she could be depressed. I thought to myself, "How sad, this poor child so needs someone's loving touch...she must have been hurt real bad sometime." Then I told her about the therapeutic touch , of how that can be of help without ever coming into contact with her body. If you should run into a person who is that threatened by physical touch, the best thing you can do is to respect his/her wishes and try to show that you care in some other way.

One of the groups in our society who are often deprived of human touch are the elderly. Perhaps, you could offer a healing t ouch to them. That could be your ministry. Take a look at the patients in a nursing home. There they are, alone in their wheel chairs or trapped in a bed, with little or no hugs or healing hands to touch them and make them feel good. Many of these senior citizens live alone and could use a visit or a phone call.

Touch is important to lovers. The song, "He Touched Me" speaks of how just a simple touch of the beloved can make a person feel overwhelmed with deep feelings. My wife, Joan, used to say to me, "Do me", when she wanted me to move my hands gently over her back. She first used the expression with her mother when she was a small child. She just loved to have her back gone over, not really massaged, but barely touched... and she never could get too much of that treatment.

She was never hesitant to ask for that kind of touch, but unfortunately many of us have those desires and never express them to our mates. There needs to be more honesty between couples. A woman should be free to express what she likes and also should feel free to say what she does not like. Of course, that should be true of the man as well. Why should two people go through years of living together without receiving or giving the kind of touch that pleases them, that is nourishing to them?

I say to you all of you to hug those special people in your lives - put your arms around them, walk with them. Continue to be lovers as you grow older, holding hands and sitting side by side, touching one another". Also hug your children and let them know the warmth of your body. Do not forget your parents and your grandparents and let them get the "feel" of you. That is one way that you can give a "healing touch". At the same time you will get the "feel" of them and be nourished as well. You become a healer when you put touch to use.

In marriage wives and husbands take turns nursing each other in times of sickness. It may be that the wife/mother is the primary healer in society. At least she is the most frequent agent giving the healing touch. That does not rule out the husband/father, for in some cases he will assume the healer's role in a home.

When we think of healers, the images that come to mind are those of doctors, nurses, religious healers or psychic healers. However, we should not overlook our role as healers in marriage. When I was doing my wife's back I was also being her healer. Though I have had a healing ministry for years I have used the healing touch in my home more than any other place. You should accept healing as one of your functions with your family. In this book I have told you how I prayed for my children and they for me, for my wife and she for me as a normal part of our family life. When someone comes to me for prayer in behalf of someone in her family, I bless her hands and pray that God will use them as healing hands with that loved one.

My message in this chapter is my conviction that in some way we are all called to be healers. In the hospital with a sick person the role is obvious, so we tend to limit healing to those who specialize in the healing arts.

When we do that we limit our opportunities for healing. We must see the larger picture. Grandpa gives a little child a memory of warmth and security as she is cradled on his warm, soft belly. Your mother's hand on your head may be every bit as helpful to you as the doctor's pill. The feel of your loved one's embrace becomes the reason you choose to live.

Never rule yourself out as a healer. In a crisis do not be afraid to act, to pray, to give the healing touch . Someone needs you...so do something about it!

Chapter 13

Keeping in Touch

I'd like to introduce you to my friend, Lloyd. He is the kind of person that Bernie Siegel would refer to as an "Exceptional Patient" - a survivor. A few years ago when he and his wife were in Florida enjoying a winter vacation he became ill. Cancer was suspected and after intensive examinations the grim verdict was in. The doctor told him there was nothing he could do, that the best thing for Lloyd to do was to go home and get his things in order - that he only had a few months to live.

I asked Lloyd, "How did you handle that shocking news?"

"Why, I got mad! Yes, that doctor really made me mad...who did he think I was?...I'm not ready to die - I'll show him...I'm going to get better, I'm going to lick this thing !"

How did he plan to lick that thing? Prayer therapy was one way. That is why he was talking to me. He had already spent quite a bit of time reading about healing and knew the value of faith and positive thought for good health. He planned to spend a lot of time reading and rereading books that would keep his mind on the right track. He would observe good health habits in matters of diet and exercise.

Then he would take time to meditate and to use visualization as a means of seeing his tumor shrink away.

He would see a little creature chewing away at his tumor in a screen in his mind. I prayed for him there in his home and suggested that he go to the Order of St. Luke healing service held weekly at our church.

When he showed up at our healing service I decided to offer him those things we had available, anointing, the laying on of hands and soaking prayer by the group. I went to him where he sat in the church pew and anointed him with oil and then I blessed him, using the therapeutic touch, which I refer to as the showers of blessings, and finally laid my hands on his head with prayer. Usually. I might use but one of these methods, but knowing the circumstances of the doctor's prediction, I thought that the "shot-gun" approach was in order. That is why I then asked him to come forward to the chancel area and sit in a chair where a group of people could pray for him. I first heard the term "soaking prayer" from Francis McNutt in his book Healing', in which he explained it to be a method of praying by a group that could spend an adequate amount of time with a patient. As the members of the prayer team gathered around him, touching him, each prayed quietly in his/her own way. Some were in total silence while others used their prayer language, another way to describe speaking in *tongues* and occasionally individuals would take turns saying a prayer out loud, when so inspired.

In group therapy some things have been learned about ways to make the prayer more effective. It adds to the strength of the group to have one member who has been healed of the same affliction as the patient. We always want at least one person who truly loves the sick person, a close member of the family or a dear friend. It is good to have both men and women in the group if that is possible to bring in the unique contribution that comes from each sex. It does not seem appropriate to involve someone who is negative about the process or thinks it would be better for the sick person to die, for that result in prayer intentions with conflicting messages. That is the reverse of the situation I mentioned earlier, when a person is being helped through the dying process only to have some individuals insisting on a physical healing.

When we are using that approach to healing prayer it is customary to inquire of the patient what is happening, what he/she is feeling. If there has been pain, is it lessening? If there has been a stiffness in a joint, is there greater mobility now? The responses of the sick person can guide the prayer group in their process and give them all cause for rejoicing when they learn that their efforts are bearing fruit. After the OSL (Order of St. Luke) group had been with Lloyd for a while, ministering to him, I asked him what he felt.

As he looked at me with tears in his eyes, his voice broke as he said, " Love... that's what it feels like...it's the most warming and loving feeling I have ever experienced".

The group approach to healing provides the most vital quality for a proper healing climate, unconditional love. Also the prayer group becomes a power house of energy as they become "one in the Spirit" with each other and with God. The prayer group provides a place for persons to try out their healing skills. As members of a group they can get used to praying for others. They may find themselves a bit nervous when they offer their first prayer aloud but in time they become skilled with experience. Some are truly gifted. That is another reason why we need prayer groups in our churches - to provide a place where those with healing gifts can have a ministry. That is where the Order of St. Luke groups can help. The OSL welcomes people who feel called to healing ministries. Without leaving their own churches they can join an OSL group and share in its healing work. Some of them come to us from churches where their pastors are not receptive to spiritual healing. Others may believe in healing but may feel uncomfortable having lay persons "doing their job", so they never get a chance to use their healing gifts.

Many pastors are trying to take care of the needs of their congregations all by themselves. They have the misguided belief that they must do it all..."that's what I'm paid for." They need to discover the great value of devout lay persons, who can supplement the pastor's work by serving as healing ministers in hospitals and on prayer teams. They will find that their own effectiveness is increased when they are backed up by that kind of a support group. Doctors also need to recognize the same thing, that those providing spiritual therapy and other support groups like Dr. Siegel's ECaP groups and Hospice groups are giving vital assistance to them as they work with their patients.

Lloyd continued to come to our weekly services for his loving treatments of soaking prayer. He spent his time as he said he would in spiritual pursuits like prayer, meditation, visualization and more reading. We started to get some good reports like, "The tumor seems to be getting smaller" and at the same time, "he's getting relief from nausea and pain." Then we received a real lift when we heard, "Lloyd was out in his boat over the weekend." Months later he went to Seattle for an intensive physical examination and evaluation of his condition. We all cheered when we finally received a call from Lloyd's wife, Margaret, informing us that "the tests were great and they have verified that the tumor has disappeared."

In the beginning, when Lloyd was first told of the gravity of his condition he felt that he still had a choice. He could go home and prepare for death or he could work to become a survivor. I feel certain that the majority of those receiving that kind of dire news from their doctor would have done their best not to disappoint him by dying some time close to the predicted date. That was not so with Lloyd, for he was an Exceptional Patient. As Dr. Siegel told us, exceptional patients will not accept a bad diagnosis...they get mad. These are people who have more things to do in this life. They want to live to be 100. They are fighters who are determined to win.

As I described Lloyd's story, did you notice that the methods we were using were the intuitive, right-brain functions? As the healing therapists, we centered-in as we prayed, asking for the healing gifts of the Spirit to flow through us. Lloyd used his inner resources as he prayed and meditated. He used his creative, right-brain functions in visualizing the tumor as shrinking in his imagination. In addition, his intuition encouraged him by giving him that knowing feeling that he would be healed.

It is my firm belief that the reason why we do not have more healings is that we do not let them happen. It is not because we do not have the potential. Many times healings do not take place because we sabotage the healing process that is going on within us. If we go along

150

with a dismal prognosis of our condition without fighting back, if we choose to die because we live without hope and it is easier to die than to cope with our problems, then we are the problem. Because of our poor attitudes, we are inhibiting all of the healing processes in us that are working hard to restore us to health. We all know about the antibodies and white blood cells that are combating the invading germs or viruses in our systems, but most of the time we are completely unaware of the mental and spiritual resources at our call in an instant. In the same way that thoughts and feelings can make us sick, thoughts and feelings can also make us well. If being spiritually ill from guilt can make us seriously sick in the body, then being healed in the spirit by forgiveness can restore the body back to health. Not only do we need to let it happen. We must fight back and make it happen - just like Lloyd did.

I hope that in the previous pages I have given you enough examples of the marvels of touch to make you want to put touch to use in the service of others. Born with a magic touch, you used it when you were a baby and throughout your childhood up until the time you were taught to concentrate on the finite world of your conscious mind. Even then God got through to you occasionally when your unconscious mind spoke to you in your dreams and when you allowed yourself to be alone to day-dream and to use your imagination in a creative way. Your interest in spiritual things has given you an awareness that the real you is not confined to your body alone but has other dimensions which scarcely know the limits of space and time.

Going within does not mean going somewhere inside your flesh and bones centered near your heart or inside your brain. "Going within" is process of reaching out to your vast unconscious mind and beyond to the one universal mind and spirit. When Jesus told us that he and the Father were one he spoke of that unity and power that comes when we get in tune with God in our inner mind. In fact, that was the key to unlock our own healing capacities. In order to "keep in touch" we need to make it a regular practice to be at one with our Lord all the time...as I stated earlier, to maintain a direct line with him at all times. St. Paul said that in a different way when he said that we must "pray without ceasing". Brother Lawrence "practiced the presence" while he was washing dishes in the monastery kitchen. You can do it while you are alone, driving your car. These are ways of "keeping in touch".

In order to be one with the Father, one with the son, one with the spirit, you must have unity within yourself. That comes when your conscious mind is in agreement with your much larger unconscious mind. Your conscious mind gets your attention most of the time. It is controlled by your Ego and is occupied with the world around you. It is the you that is impressed by things, by status and social position, by worldly achievements. It is absorbed with those things you have been taught. It relies on facts and figures and the recall of your personal experiences. As you remain in the realm of your conscious mind you feel safe because your Ego is secure. But remaining there makes you only half a person. The world may think you are great but without going within you are still shallow, living only on the surface.

Keeping in touch means opening yourself up to your inner resources and moving with the flow of the universe. It means daring to trust your intuitive nature and allowing that wisdom to lead you. God does not speak to you in your conscious mind. That mind can read books about the nature of God and it can come to the conclusion that there is a God who is a creator, that there is a Son who is a redeemer and a Spirit who is there to inspire. That does not require belief or faith. When I say I believe in God or that I believe in Jesus, I am taking a step in faith which involves commitment.

The knowing that comes when I say, I believe does not come from what you have learned in your conscious mind. That certain knowledge we call belief comes from within. When Jesus asked the disciples, "Who do men say that the Son of man is ?" and they came up with different answers, naming people like John the Baptist, Elijah and Jeremiah, they were giving logical answers from their conscious minds. But when Peter answered with, "You are the Christ, the Son of the living God," Jesus told him, "Blessed are you, Simon Bar-Jona ! For flesh and blood has not revealed this to you, but my Father who is in heaven" (Matt 16: 13-17 RSV). Peter was receiving God's inspiration through his unconscious mind. We have a unity of our minds when the conscious mind receives a thought or belief from within and accepts it as its own, as in the case of Peter above. Once revealed it became incorporated into the body of learned knowledge in his conscious mind forever.

Some of you who have been reading my book will not know what to make of some of the things I have been sharing with you. I am sure that others are gifted in some facet of healing and are reading this to pick up new ideas and perhaps, to be affirmed in their own ministries by my own witness. Some of you who are new to this may be

153

wondering about your own talents. If you are sick, can you receive help from any of the sources I have mentioned? Are you an Exceptional Patient and do you want to become a SURVIVOR?

If you are at all curious I am sure that you have done some experimenting with your right brain functions while you have been reading this book. Even as I have been telling you about my experiences I have become much more conscious of that part of my nature. Just before I arrived at this chapter I had a chance to test my intuitive gifts again.

Following our weekly OSL healing service, Jason, one of the children present, came running to me in a panic, crying out between each breath. "Father Miner.. I lost my... little silver ball...underneath the door...can you come and open it for me?" When I found out which door Jason was talking about I knew that I didn't have the key on my chain. I went into the church office and found the box containing all of the church keys. There they were, numbered 1-50, and there was not a clue to explain which door they opened.

As I picked up the box ,I said to Jason's mother, "Well, Carol, I've been writing about reaching down inside to your inner resources. Now I have the chance to see how well I can do." I examined the door to the storage room and noted that it had a keyhole in the door handle and above it another keyhole for a deadbolt lock. I tried to "tune in" as I gazed at the assortment of keys. Finally deciding on number 23. I put it into the door handle and "what do you know?" it worked! Next was the deadbolt, so I figured logically that it should be the next key, number 24. Not so, it did not fit. My next logical step was to try the next key in the other direction, number 22 and that time the deadbolt lock opened.

You can imagine how relieved I was. It was an effective demonstration of the value of our intuitive resources and in addition, it spared me the ordeal of trying out twenty two keys with little Jason dancing up and down, waiting for his ball. In relating this to my son, Phil, he asked me if I had ever used that key before, the first one I picked. I thought about it for awhile and then said, "Yes, I may have used it before, but it's been years since I ever needed to get into that room. Why do you ask?" "Dad, you know that our subconscious mind remembers everything. Yours probably recognized that key." I really believe that is what happened. That inner mind was able to "zero in" on key number 23 because there was something recognizable about it. Just think of all the other things that mind remembers !

And your mind works the same way !

That wonderful resource works for us in the healing ministry. Those who have read, *Healing is for Real* [2] will remember that my first impressive healing of a dying woman coming out of a coma back to health, came when I knew very little about the subject of healing. I relied on another person's faith (the daughter of the sick woman) and simple trust and the woman was healed. If I had relied on my logic in that instance, perhaps the lady would have died, because I did not think healing prayer would work. But someone else did, and I was able to turn off my conscious mind and let my intuitive resources go to work as I laid hands on her with a simple prayer.

Are you ready to step forth and do the same? If you

are a nurse, will you try the "therapeutic touch" ? If you are a clergy person, are you willing to be a healing pastor ? If you are a medical doctor, are you willing to be personal with your patients and let them dare to hope ? If you have empathy for the dying, will you consider volunteering for a Hospice group ? What about you lay persons ? Do you not know that we have all been called to this ministry ? What will be your role ? Are you ready to offer the healing touch to someone in need? Perhaps you might like to join a prayer group. What about you people who have been described as seriously ill? Why not work at being a survivor and join an ECaP group or something similar? There is a place for any of you who are reading these words. If you are a just a spectator, perhaps it is time you got into the game. That is where the real satisfaction is to be found... and the beauty of it is this - that when you become one with the father and have compassion upon his children that you too will do great works of healing.

Along with the positive attitude I have been presenting in this work, I must address the idea of *redemptive suffering* , briefly mentioned previously. For many centuries illness was considered a means God used to test us. In the Roman Catholic Church that was one of the measures of sainthood, the willingness for an individual to offer his/her suffering to the Lord. There has been an emphasis on self-denial and suffering in many of the world's religions. The prominent example in the Old Testament was the case of Job, who steadfastly withstood the test of the afflictions sent to him by his God. Then there is Jesus, who is the great example for all Christians. Even non-Christians, like Gandhi were influenced by his example. Jesus did call his followers to a life of service and sacrifice. As a result, there are those today who after doing all they could to regain their health, have come to see their plight as an opportunity for redemptive suffering, the willful offering of their pain and sickness to God as an act of service and devotion. That appears to be another valid way to deal with suffering. There have been times in my ministry that I wondered why some of the most saintly persons were not healed. It seemed to me that those persons must fit into the category of redemptive suffering. I also observed that as their bodies continued to deteriorate that another kind of healing was at work, one of mind and spirit - perhaps the greatest healing we can hope for !

Remember that even in these cases, your touch can heal.

Chapter 14

The Bottom Line - Forgiveness

I believe that the most important factor in healing is forgiveness. Our bodies become vulnerable to sickness when we are off-balance on the spiritual level. In order to become whole spiritually we must be free from the four blocks to healing mentioned in Chapter 6: fear, hate, guilt and inferiority feelings.

Through God's compassion and love we can eliminate every one of those negatives - and the means of doing this is forgiveness. To be forgiven is to know the love of God which takes away the fear. In the first Epistle of John we read, "God is love. Whoever lives in love lives in God, and God in him...There is no fear in love. But perfect love drives out fear" (1 John 4: 16-18 . Likewise, there is no room in a forgiving heart for anger, resentment or bitterness - so that addresses the second inhibiter of healing, hate. It has been suspected that unresolved hurts and resentments, stored in the unconscious mind, may be the root cause of diseases like cancer and arthritis. We have long known that hypertension, which can cause strokes and heart attacks is often the result of stress. A mind full of loving thoughts, a mind at peace with oneself and with others can be the beginning of health in all other areas of one's life.

Guilt enters the picture and takes away from us our feeling of oneness with God. We no longer feel safe in his love because we believe that we have done something displeasing to Him and that has made Him angry. That feeling separates us from the One we knew as a loving God. Because we went against his will and were unkind to someone - because we have been unloving to others in our thoughts and in our actions, we feel alienated from God. He is no longer our refuge but the One who will punish us - the very object of our fear. We believe that we deserve to be punished because of our offenses. When we get to that state we become wide open to the assaults of disease and the pain and suffering associated with it. Now guilt is in charge. We are overcome with feelings that we are bad, unworthy of anyone's love, especially God's. That allows the fourth inhibiter of healing, inferiority feelings, to enter the picture and make us feel that we are inadequate persons, no good - wretched souls, not worth saving - not worth healing. That is how it is when we feel separated from God. We say that we " feel like hell", a statement which sums up our situation accurately. For that is what hell is all about - the belief that we are alone, apart from others and from God: Only the knowledge that we are forgiven can bring us to wholeness again.

Dr. Gerald Jampolsky has dealt with this same subject in his book, titled *Good-bye to Guilt*. In the first chapter, entitled, "Forgiveness Heals and Ends the Game of Guilt" he cites fear as the major barrier to health and wholeness.

"Our biggest obstacle to experiencing peace of mind, or oneness with love, is our fear of God. Because we believe we are separate from God, we feel guilty and in conflict and competition with each other - and that is the bottom line of all our difficulties regardless of their nature. Healing is a process through which our mind is cleansed of its negative thoughts of fear and guilt - all those condemning judgments that make us feel vulnerable, separate and fragmented. Forgiveness is the means by which this process is accomplished. It permits the mind, that misperceives and sees itself as split and separate, to be made whole." [1]

Maybe you feel that you are too far gone - too unlovable - too incorrigible to qualify for God's love and forgiveness ? Not so. When one has encountered one or all four of the inhibiters to healing, fear, hate, guilt and inferiority feelings, it is difficult to him/her to believe that forgiveness is possible. Often, religious leaders have overemphasized judgment to the extent of obscuring Christ's teachings on love and forgiveness. The central theme in the message of Jesus is the "Good News" of God's love. Over and over, he not only taught of God's love for us, he demonstrated it in his living, making his final act the supreme gift of his own life for us. The Gospels are full of examples of God's love for the unlovable. In the fifteenth chapter of St. Luke, Jesus tells the story of the Prodigal Son to show the true forgiving nature of God (Luke 15: 11-31). I should like to point out that even though it is "the father" who represents God in this story. It is a father who is unafraid to use the feminine within him as he deals with his arrant son.

The story of the Prodigal Son is one of the most popular of Jesus' parables. However, in spite of its popularity, few realize that it is a story about God and us. It is not just a story of this family who lived in a past time - but it is a story of unconditional love. It is a story which tells us what kind of God we have. I suggest that you read it for yourself. Put yourself in the place of each of the characters, the erring Prodigal, the Elder brother and the Father. Sense how each one feels and see where you can identify with each one. Which one do you relate to today? Are you the Prodigal? Are you the Elder Brother? Do you know that, eventually, you must be able to choose the position of the Father for yourself?

To refresh your memory, let me give you the salient points of the story. Somewhere back in those Biblical times there lived a farmer and his two sons. The younger of the two approached his father with the unthinkable suggestion that he give him his inheritance right away. In a way, it was like saying, "Father, I can't wait for you to die!

I want what is mine now!"

Perhaps, what was more amazing was the fact that the father complied with the youth's wishes. Keep in mind that Jesus was presenting the father as one who behaved the same as God would do. Just as the younger son was given the freedom to do as he pleased, also we are given free choice over our life's decisions. One of the gifts of God is our freedom to make our own mistakes.

In our story the young man took advantage of that freedom. He went off to a typical Canaanite city, noted for its wild life and managed to go through all of his inheritance in short time. In our time we can conceive of someone going to Las Vegas and gambling away his entire fortune. After he had been there for some time that country was engulfed in a severe depression and eventually the young man was truly destitute. He was

161

reduced to making his living feeding pigs. He even craved to eat the food being given to the pigs, but none was offered to him.

He was feeling sorry for himself and thought of how good things had been at home. He compared himself to his father's servants. He said, "How many of my father's hired men have food to spare, and here I am starving to death.". Because of his need he decided to return home. But how could he show up there after failing so miserably as a son - as a brother - as a person. He must humble himself and make a demonstration of repentance. He would say, "Father, I have sinned against heaven and against you. I am no longer worthy to be called your son; make me like one of your hired men". I really believe that he was motivated to do this more out of his need than his repentant feelings He set out on his homeward journey and as he approached the family homestead an incredible thing happened.

Before he could approach his father and give his rehearsed speech, the old man made the first move. While he was still a long way off, his father saw him and was filled with compassion for him; he ran to his son, threw his arms around him and kissed him . The son had not yet uttered his statement of remorse. It was only after that loving greeting on the part of the father that the Prodigal gave his speech in which he confessed his unworthiness.

Even then, the father chose to ignore what the son was saying as he cried, "Quick! Bring the best robe and put it on him. Put a ring on his finger and sandals on his feet. Bring the fatted calf and kill it. Let's have a feast and celebrate".

Most of our religious teachings emphasize the necessity of our making the first move towards reconciliation - but here we have God (being portrayed in this story as the father) reaching out in forgiving love even before the son had an opportunity to make his act of repentance. That is what unconditional love is all about. In this story, Jesus not only told us what our heavenly Father is like, but also showed us the way we should behave towards others. As God's children we too should reach out to those who have offended us and offer them our forgiveness. It proves to be the way to our own forgiveness. In the Lord's Prayer, Jesus taught us to say, "Forgive us our trespasses as we forgive those who trespass against us".(Matt 6: 12). In the next passage, Jesus emphasized the importance of forgiving others so that we too might be forgiven. "For if you forgive men when they sin against you, your heavenly Father will also forgive you (Matt: 6:14). The bottom line for healing is forgiveness. Likewise the bottom line in receiving forgiveness is forgiving others. The very best thing you can do for yourself is to offer your forgiveness for others - even if you do not think that they deserve it - even if they are still unforgiving to you. Even when you are not feeling like it, but you are willing to have it done, God will accept your intention and you will be forgiven.

The story of the Prodigal Son is not over when the son is received into his father's arms. The elder brother, who was out in the fields, working, heard the music, the singing and dancing and asked one of the servants what was happening. When he found out that the party was being held in honor of his younger brother he was furious. He refused to enter the house and remained outside to show his displeasure. His father pleaded with him to come in but he retorted: "Look, all these years

163

I've been slaving for you and never disobeyed your orders. Yet you never gave me even a young goat so I could celebrate with my friends. But when this son of yours who has squandered your property with prostitutes comes home, you kill the fattened calf for him" (Luke 15:29).

It really is not difficult to understand the viewpoint of the older brother. In the name of fairness, he seems to present a good case. But here we are not dealing with the world's standards, we are dealing with God's. From our point of view, the father (God) does not appear to be fair. Obviously, the younger son needs to be punished, while at the same time, his older brother should be rewarded.

Unconditional love is difficult for most human beings to handle. After being taught of the need for punishment for our misdeed or errors we do not want to see anyone else get away with anything. Most of the time we practice conditional love with others - with our children, our mates, our siblings - even our parents. i will love you if you behave the way i want you to - when you get good grades - when you clean up your room - when what you do reflects well on me. No wonder we sympathize with the older brother!

However, what we are overlooking is what God sees in us at all times - our intrinsic worth. He created us as his own and endowed each of us with potentials and values not easily seen by the world. He desires that we be our total creative selves, living abundant lives - seeing ourselves as heirs of God and co-creators with him. That younger child had died to all of that potential. He had come to live without hope. But now he had returned from the dead as the father expressed it to his faithful, hard-working son.

"My son, you are always with me, and everything I have is yours. But we had to celebrate and be glad, because this brother of yours was dead and is alive again; he was lost and is found"(Luke 15: 31).

Learning to forgive is learning to become like the father in the above story. It takes effort to learn forgiveness. It helps when we know that when others are aggressive towards us and attack us, that they are revealing their fears and feelings of low esteem. What we see in them as bad are often projections of our own inadequacies foisted on them. Sometimes, if we visualize them as they were when they were children, it becomes easier to deal with them without judging. We can stop this cycle of attack-counter attack by taking on the Father's role and reaching out with compassion and offering love to assuage their fear.

Even the Elder Son in each of us needs love and forgiveness and in the story, the Father gave him assurances of that love. Sometimes, because we feel we have been good we become guilty of judging others. It is easy to do. But when we do it, isn't it nice to know that God applies the same healing forgiveness to us as well.

To be a healer or to be healed one must start out clean. We have to begin and end our healing process the same way by forgiving. Remember, the bottom line is forgiveness! When you have forgiveness, your touch can heal!

APPENDIX

How to use the Healing Touch

In offering yourself as a healer you must be true to yourself. Each one of us has gifts that are unique to us. I cannot tell you what to do - I can only suggest things for you to try. Trust your inner guide as you work with someone in need and act with authority which comes from identifying with your higher power.

The first thing we need to do is to tune in. Before applying any techniques using your mind or your healing touch, it is important to clear yourself from all external distractions. You want to be a clear channel of God's grace so you must take care that you have no negative feelings due to hostility or resentment, Bring forgiveness into your consciousness and make sure that you have a forgiving attitude towards all others. Then, do as Jesus did so often, look with compassion upon the sick person. Bring love into the sickroom.

There is no one way to pray for healing. I use the word pray to describe what we do whether we say words out loud or not for I believe that every time we have an intention - a hope or desire to achieve something, we are praying. We may not consciously direct our thoughts to God as we know him , but whenever there is an urgency to accomplish a certain end we automatically use all the resources we have available to us. Our Inner Guide will go into action as soon as we have a need. When we have come to know our resource as Holy Spirit, or Jesus, or the Christ Within, we may appropriately address him by name. Those in the 12-Step programs will acknowledge that great results are achieved when your resource has no other name than "Higher Power." In other traditions the connection is achieved when those believers make their appeal in the name of their own spiritual resource. I believe that God is attuned to all of his children no matter which channel they may use to reach him.

Approach the sick person with confidence. If it were all up to you, you might have reason to doubt. However, it is not all up to you. In spiritual healing you are relying upon the higher power. It is important for you to let go and allow your Inner Guide to direct you through the healing process. Put your Ego to the side and let the Spirit form your words and move your hands to where they should apply the healing touch. If you have been called to someone's home or to the hospital begin to prepare yourself for the encounter as you travel. As a Christian I invite Jesus to go with me and to be by my side as I offer my ministry to the sick person. I always have the philosophy that I must be Jesus - do what he would do for the one in need. Whatever your belief system may be (and we all have one), you must appeal to the Highest Good to lead you.

As you prepare in advance you may feel some sensations in your hands, such as heat or a tingling feeling. Once you have arrived at the sickroom make certain that the patient knows who you are and why you have come to see her. Sometimes friends of the sick person think it is a good idea for you to apply your ministrations and ask you to go, without notifying the patient. If the patient shows any apprehension and does not want your help, do honor her request and leave. We should never be in the position of forcing ourselves on the hapless patient, regardless of how much good we feel we can do. However, most of the time you will be given a hearty welcome by the one who is ailing. Already she has been poked at, punctured with needles, fed a variety of pills, has been taken to X-ray and has lain there in distress as her medical team has stood over her bed and discussed her condition. In contrast, you seem to be someone on her side - a friendly face from some other place. She is looking to you as a relief from this misery. Maybe with a simple word or touch you may be able to take away the pain and cause healing to happen quickly and indeed, you may. On the other hand, what you may do may not be apparent at all. What you can do is to bring love to the room and with it hope and encouragement. You may not always be able to heal the patient's physical condition but you can always leave their room filled with warmth and light.

The following are examples of different situations which one might find in practicing the healing touch therapy. As each case differs from all others, the healing therapist must be flexible enough to adapt to the unique needs of the one in need. That is why the healing touch ministry relies so heavily upon the intuitive method of going within. After gaining some experience the spiritual healer becomes better able to discern the right actions for the given situation.

LAYING ON OF HANDS

SITUATION 1: The sick person is in bed in a hospital room. She/he is there for diagnosis and treatment. You do not need to know all the particulars about the case.

You are there to treat the patient, not the disease so your approach is to the person.

WHAT TO DO: Approach the person and make yourself known if you have not already met. Briefly explain that you are there at his/her own request and that you are pleased to offer your LOH therapy. Depending on the patient's background. such as membership in a church, you will know if it is appropriate to pray out loud. It is not necessary to appeal to your higher power with words, but when requested, it can be most comforting to the sick person. For the laying on of hands you may stand over the bed and gently place your hands on the patient's head. As you do this, tune in to the God of the Universe and become connected with him and all of creation. You do not have to do anything to the sick person. You merely release him/her to the healing Lord, asking for health and wholeness. After a brief time you might ask the patient what is happening. Is she/he feeling anything special? Is there pain somewhere? If the patient feels heat or a vibration tell him/her that is normal, that something good is taking place. Be sensitive to the voice within and when you feel it is right, bring your treatment to a close. Also, be sensitive to the patient's religious preference. For those I know to be Christians, I offer the prayers in the name of Jesus Christ. If I knew that the patient were Jewish, I might offer the prayer in the name of the God of Abraham or Moses. With some the words;' higher power' might be more fitting... with some, no words at all. I often ask a family member such as the husband or wife to join me in the healing touch by taking the patients hand as I pray. It helps them to feel useful as they share in the healing process. It's similar to their lighting a candle for the sick person. They are doing something!

SITUATION II: A healing service where people are asked to come forward to receive the laying on of hands with a group. That would usually be offered after a talk on the subject of healing.

WHAT TO DO: Those with some need of healing come forward and either stand, sit or kneel to receive the healing ministrations. Most often this kind of healing touch is administered by two or more persons. The healee is asked what is wrong. The need may be anything from chronic arthritis, cancer, back ache to a request for help in a marriage and in some cases, a call for forgiveness. One person leads the questioning and directs the healing response. Usually, a word of advice is given and when appropriate, assurance of forgiveness is offered. It is very important to address the matter of forgiveness, for as I said in Chapter 14, that the bottom line in all healing is forgiveness. The counseling is followed by the laying on of hands by the group members, who remain silent as the leader prays aloud. It is also all right to do all of this in silence. The same principle is involved: God is the healer and we do not need to tell him what to do. We merely offer our sick person to the great healer.

SITUATION III: The patient is quite ill and probably needs to be in bed or in a chair. The condition is either chronic or the sick person has been under treatment for some time.

WHAT TO DO: One method is called Soaking Prayer, a method suggested by Francis MacNutt? A number of persons are willing to stay in an attitude of prayer and healing for a lengthy period of time. Periodically the

170

patient is asked how she/he is feeling and then prayer is resumed again. Most of the praying is done in silence. It is not unusual to hear some persons praying in tongues if that is a part of their tradition.

THERAPEUTIC TOUCH:

SITUATION I : Person in hospital bed following surgery that day. She/he is in pain and finds conversation difficult. Need is for healing of the bodily wounds, rest and removal of pain.

WHAT TO DO: As before with the LOH, begin by tuning in to God and the Universe. Dolores Krieger calls this centering in in her book on the Therapeutic Touch, which is an excellent resource on this method. Once you feel you are in harmony and have a peaceful feeling inside yourself, begin moving yours hands over the person's body from head to foot, keeping five or six inches from the sick person. Keeping your hands totally relaxed, let them find their way over the area of need. After going the length and breadth of the body your hands will detect heat in certain places. That is the area of the incision. Once you have felt the heat, continue to move your hands there until the feeling of heat subsides. Often, while you are doing this, the patient will interject, "What are you doing? It feels good and the pain is going away". I find that when the therapeutic touch therapy is over that the patient has completely relaxed and asleep, at which point I quietly leave the room.

SITUATION II: You are on a picnic and one of the softball players turns his ankle and it has begun to swell and he is in great pain.

WHAT TO DO: As in the case above, begin by tuning in and while the patient's foot is raised, begin the therapeutic touch motion, going back and forth over the swollen area. You should begin this as soon as possible after the accident occurred. I find that when I have finished with the therapeutic touch it is also good to apply my hands directly over the afflicted except if there is an open wound. In all accidents follow all the recommended procedures of the Red Cross for First Aid before your touch therapy. In general, I have had positive results in using the therapeutic touch for bruises or sprains. The first sign of improvement noticed is the reduction of pain, often followed by a significant reduction in the swelling .

SITUATION III: Cases of sunburn and also the more serious burns are commonplace and usually very painful.

WHAT TO DO: Follow the same procedures as described in the cases above. The great advantage of the therapeutic touch method in dealing with burn victims is the fact that no physical contact is made with the burned area of the person's body. Though therapy by physicians is usually needed, it is my belief that the healing touch facilitates healing for those who suffer from burns.

172

ANOINTING WITH OIL

SITUATION: Persons requesting Sacramental rites of healing through the Church's ministry in cases of illness, including the last rites.

WHAT TO DO: Holy Unction is a Sacrament, administered only by priests in the Roman Catholic and Anglican Churches. For many years it was referred to as Extreme Unction and was given only to the dying as the Last Sacrament in the Roman Catholic Church. Recently, it has been restored as a rite used for healing. It has become popular in the Episcopal Church to offer anointing in conjunction with the Holy Eucharist, usually advertised as a healing service in the middle of the week. At that service the priest dips his thumb into the holy oil and makes the sign of the cross on the sick person's forehead. I am sure that a similar practice is done by ministers of other persuasions. The use of oil for healing is an ancient practice in the Christian Church and is referred to in the Epistle of James in the New Testament (James 5:14). In addition to the Church's sacrament there is a general use of applying oil for healing done by lay persons. Oil which has been prayed over is shared with the members of a healing group. There is no special way to use this oil for healing. People use it creatively, to bless those who are sick and sometimes use it on their bodies in a gentle massage.

PRAYERS FOR ANOINTING:

N., I anoint you with oil in the Name of the Father, and of the Son, and of the Holy Spirit (or in the Name of God).

The following may be added
As you are outwardly anointed with this holy oil, so may our heavenly Father grant you the inward anointing of the Holy Spirit. Of his great mercy, may he forgive you your sins, release you from suffering, and restore you to wholeness and strength. May he deliver you from all evil, preserve you in all goodness and bring you to everlasting life; through Jesus Christ our Lord. Amen (Book of Common Prayer, p.456)

N., I anoint you with oil in the Name of God, asking for your healing in mind, body and spirit. Amen

GROUP PRAYERS FOR HEALING

SITUATION I: Prayer at a distance: the sick person or persons not present, called Intercessory Prayer.

WHAT TO DO: One person may lead the prayers, e.g. a minister in a church, naming those who are sick in the presence of the congregation. Another kind of prayer ministry is done by a Prayer Group, who meet regularly for study, meditation and intercessory prayer. They compile a list of those who have needs - physical, mental, emotional or spiritual. Someone in the group

174

presents the names of the sick persons and may explain something of the need. It is a good idea not to dwell on these bits of information as there is a danger of getting involved in gossip, particularly in cases such as marital problems. The members of the Prayer Group agree to pray daily for all those on the list. One pleasant part of the gathering is learning of the improvements and healings of those who have been prayed for. Such groups as these develop strong and meaningful relationships among the members. There are hundreds of such groups around the world, each ready to testify to the effectiveness of Intercessory Prayer.

SITUATION II: People at a gathering, where some of them express the need for different kinds of healing.

WHAT TO DO: A common method is to have the needy person stand or sit in the middle of a circle, formed by those present. In different ways the group members offer their love and energy to the ones in the center. Sometimes touch is used and those present may offer "hugs" to the ones with problems. Another method is to divide in twos and take turns being the healer and the healee as everyone sits in silence. When taking the part of the healer a person will offer his/her compassion and caring thoughts and feelings as they sit together in an attitude of prayer.

SITUATION III: People everywhere are in need of the healing touch as they go through life seeking wholeness.

WHAT TO DO: Be there for them when they need the assurance of physical contact. Our need starts in infancy and continues into old age. Being held is such a comfort to a child - and we usually are there to do it for our children and grandchildren. However, as life goes on we tend to distance ourselves from others, even sometimes in families. Let us not be afraid to use the healing touch we call a hug frequently with our families and friends . And let us not forget the lonely elders in our midst - they need hugs too! The healing touch comes in many forms but in every case, it is an expression of love.

SUGGESTED PRAYERS AND BLESSINGS

(Offer each from the heart and with authority).

Mizpah Blessing: The Lord watch between you and me, when we are absent one from the other. (Genesis 31:49)

May the Lord bless, you and keep you now and forever. Amen.

The blessing of God, Father, Son and Holy Spirit be with you now and remain with you forever. Amen

I (we) lay hands on you in the name of the Healing Christ that you may be healed. Amen.
We appeal to Raphael, the healing angel to assist us in our need.

Finally: Be creative and make your words according to your own belief system, be it Christian, Jewish, Buddhist, Islam, Hindu, Bahia, or your own "Higher Power".

CHAPTER NOTES

Chapter 1

1. Lewis Thomas, *The Lives of a Cell* (New York: Viking Press, 1974)

2. Joseph Chilton Pearce, *Magical Child* (New York: E.P. Dutton, 1977).

Chapter 3

1. Glen Clark, *I will lift up Mine Eyes,* (New York, Harper & Row, 1937).

Chapter 4

1. Fritz Kunkel, *Creation Continues ,* (Waco, Texas: WordBooks, 1973).

Chapter 5

1. William Blatty, *The Exorcist,* (New York: Harper & Row, 1971

2. Linn and Linn, *Deliverance Prayer,* (New York: Paulist Press, 1981).

3. Kenneth McAll, *Healing the Family Tree,* (London: Sheldon Press 1982).

4. Edith Fiore, *The Unquiet Dead, a Psychologist Treats Spirit Possession,* (New York: Ballantine Books, Random House Inc).

Chapter 6

1. Bernie S. Siegel, *Love, Medicine & Miracles ,* (New York: Harper & Row, 1986).

2. 0. Carl Simonton, Stephanie Matthews-Simonton, and James Creighton, *Getting Well Again,* (Los Angeles: J.P. Tarcher, 978, New York: Bantam, 1980).

3. Gerald Jampolsky, *Love is Letting go of Fear,* (Millbrae, CA.: Celestial Arts, 1979).

4. William R.Parker and Elaine St. John, *Prayer Can Change Your Life,* (Cannel, N.Y.: Guideposts, 1957).

5. John A. Sanford, *Dreams: God's Forgotten Language,* (New York: Lippencott Co., 1968).

6. Malcolm H. Miner, *Healing and the Abundant Life,* (Wilton, CT.:

177

Morehouse-Barlow Co.,1979). Reprinted as *Living with the Rejoice Plan,* (Anchorage, Alaska: Rejoice Publications 1987).

Chapter 8

1. Dolores Krieger, *The Therapeutic Touch,* (Englewood N.J.: Prentice Hall, Inc., 1979).

2. Bernie S. Siegel, *Love, Medicine & Miracles,* p.32.

Chapter 9

1. Mary Jane Linn, Matthew Linn, Dennis Linn, *Healing the Dying,* (New York: Paulist Press, 1979).

2. Elisabeth Kubler-Ross, *On Death and Dying,* (New York: MacMillan Co).

3. Sogyal Rinpoche, *The Tibetan Book of Living and Dying,* (Harper San Fracisco,1992)

Chapter 10

1. John A. Sanford, *Healing and Wholeness,* (New York: Paulist Press, 1977).

2. Jean M. Auel, *The Clan of the Cave Bear,* (New York: Crown Publishers).

3.Malcolm H. Miner, *Healing and the Abundant Life,* Chapter 11.

Chapter 11

1. John Wesley, *"The Journal of the Rev. John Wesley",* (Volumes covering the years 1736-1790).

2. Morton Kelsey, *Healing and Christianity,* (New York: Harper & Row, 1973).

Chapter 13

1. **Francis MacNutt,** *Healing,* (Noire Dame, Ind.: Ave Maria Press, 1974).

2. Malcolm H. Miner, *Healing is for Real,* (Wilton, CT Morehouse-Barlow Co, 1972).

Chapter 14

1. Gerald Jampolsky, *Goodbye to Guilt*
(New York, N.Y.: Bantam Books, Inc.,1985).

Appendix

1. Francis MacNutt, Healing, Notre Dame, Ind: Ave Maria Press
1974

2. Dolores Krieger, The Therapeutic Touch, Englewood, NJ :
Prentice Hall Inc.1979.

www.ingramcontent.com/pod-product-compliance
Lightning Source LLC
LaVergne TN
LVHW011232080426
835509LV00005B/459